BECOMING

God

The Path of the
Christian Mystic

MYSTICAL PATHS OF THE WORLD'S RELIGIONS

BECOMING

God

The Path of the Christian Mystic

ELIZABETH CLARE PROPHET

SUMMIT UNIVERSITY PRESS®

Gardiner, Montana

BECOMING GOD: The Path of the Christian Mystic
by Elizabeth Clare Prophet
Copyright © 2010 Summit Publications, Inc.
All rights reserved

For information, contact Summit University Press,
63 Summit Way, Gardiner, MT 59030.
Tel: 1-800-245-5445 or 406-848-9500
Web site: www.SummitUniversityPress.com

Library of Congress Control Number 2010930399
ISBN 978-1-932890-50-1 (softbound)
ISBN 978-1-932890-84-6 (eBook)

SUMMIT UNIVERSITY ♨ PRESS

Cover design by Lynn M. Wilbert
Interior design by James Bennett Design

Printed in the United States of America
15 14 13 12 11 10   6 5 4 3 2 1

Disclaimer: No guarantee whatsoever is made to anyone by Summit University Press or Elizabeth Clare Prophet that the spiritual system of the Science of the Spoken Word, including meditation, visualization, dynamic decrees and spiritual healing, embodied in this book will yield successful results for anyone at any time. The functioning of cosmic law is a direct experience between the individual and his own higher consciousness. As in Jesus' time, some were healed and some were not—according to their faith or lack of it. Karma and the Divine Providence must be the final arbiter of each one's application of the sacred fire. We can only witness to our personal healing—body, mind and soul—through the use of the suggested mantras and spiritual disciplines. Each man may prove or disprove the Law for himself. The practice and proof of the science of being rests with the individual. No one can do it for another. These spiritual techniques do not replace medical treatment or diagnosis.

Note: Because gender-neutral language can be cumbersome and at times confusing, we have often used *he* and *him* to refer to God or the individual. These terms are for readability only and are not intended to exclude women or the feminine aspect of the Godhead. Likewise, our use of *God* or *Spirit* does not exclude other expressions for the Divine. The soul of man and woman is feminine in relation to the masculine, or spirit, portion of being. The soul is therefore often referred to as "she."

CONTENTS

PART THREE | FORMULAS FOR MYSTICAL
TRANSFORMATION

ILLUSTRATIONS

Transformation into Christ through Prayer
by Blessed Angela of Foligno (1248–1309)

It is in prayer that one finds God. There are three schools, that is, three types of prayer, without which one does not find God. These are bodily, mental, and supernatural.

Bodily prayer takes place with the sound of words and bodily movements such as genuflections. I never abandon this type of prayer. For sometimes when I want to devote myself to mental prayer, I am impeded by my laziness or by sleepiness. So I turn to bodily prayer, which leads to mental prayer. It should be done with attention. For instance, when you say the Our Father, you should weigh carefully what you are saying. Do not run through it, trying to complete a certain number of them, like little ladies doing piece work.

Prayer is mental when meditating on God so occupies the soul that one thinks of nothing but God. If some other thought comes to mind I no longer call such prayers mental. Such prayer curbs the tongue and renders one speechless. The mind is so totally filled with God's presence that it cannot think or speak about anything except about God and in God. From mental prayer, then, we move on to supernatural prayer.

I call prayer supernatural when God, bestowing this gift upon the soul and filling it with his presence, so elevates the soul that it is stretched, as it were, beyond its natural capacities. In this type of prayer, the soul understands more of God than would seem naturally possible. It knows that it cannot understand, and what it knows it cannot explain, because all that it sees and feels is beyond its own nature.

In these three schools of prayer you come to know who you are and who God is. From the fact that you know, you love. Loving, you desire to possess what you love. And this is the sign of true love: that the one who loves is transformed, not partially, but totally, into the Beloved.[1]

To Souls Yearning to Be One with God

I welcome you to explore with me the world of the Christian mystics. Mystics are those who seek a direct experience of the Presence of God. They yearn to know God, to see God and to be one with God *now*. Mysticism is not exclusive to Christianity. It is the vital, animating element at the heart of every religion. There have always been mystics, and they have always plumbed the depths and scaled the heights of the soul's potential. Mystics are *psychologists**—students of the soul intent on their spiritual quest. Their lives and teachings are a road map that leads to the very summit of being.

The aspiration of every mystic is one and the same: union with God. The mystic does not postpone his pursuit of this goal, because he cannot. Saint Teresa of Avila expressed the soul's deep yearning for God when she wrote, "I am oblivious of everything in that anxious longing to see God; that desert and solitude seem to the soul better than all the companionship of the world."[1]

---

*The term *psychology* (*psyche* 'breath, spirit, soul' + *logia* 'study of') was originally used to mean "study of the soul."

Meister Eckhart, a fourteenth century mystic and theologian, wrote: "God's being is my life, but if it is so, then what is God's must be mine and what is mine God's. God's is-ness *[istigkeit]* is my is-ness, and neither more nor less."[2]

When I was a child I was taught to believe that I was made in the image and likeness of God. Whenever I heard that statement I would think, "Well, if I'm made in the image and likeness of God, I must be God"—because there's no difference between the person and the reflection. But I talked to hundreds of people who could not see that. To make that transition, to take that next step, was blasphemy to them. And so I realized that in order for me to think my independent thoughts, I had to withdraw from most of the churches of organized religion.

The Goal of the Mystical Path

After I had the opportunity to read and research the lives of many mystics, I could see why God has called us to walk in the footsteps of the saints. The goal of becoming one with God or, as some of the mystics say, becoming God, has been a part of the Christian mystical tradition since the time of Jesus Christ. Early Christians referred to this doctrine as *deification*. But where is this teaching today? We do not hear it being preached from the pulpits.

Although volumes and volumes have been written by and about the many saints who have walked the earth, the churches are not teaching the full story of the lives of the saints or what it takes to pursue a path of sainthood all the way to union with God. They are not teaching that it is possible to be a saint and that you can pursue this path and still be a member of your family, society and the world.

In the early twentieth century, John Arintero, a Spanish theologian who sought to revive the teachings of the mystics, lamented:

"Unfortunately, these sublime and consoling doctrines [of the mystics] are utterly forgotten.... Deification, so well known to the [Church] Fathers, but unfortunately forgotten today, is the primary purpose of the Christian life."[3] Imagine if the churches were teaching today that we are intended to become God and that this is the goal of life!

Arintero also noted that the early Christians understood that their goal was to become united with Christ in such a way that they, too, would acquire divine powers. He said:

> The acts of the martyrs and the customs of the first centuries offer us interesting evidences of this fact. The Christians of those times appreciated, understood, and lived the supernatural life in such a way that they liked to be called Godbearers or Christbearers. Therefore, when [the Roman emperor] Trajan asked St. Ignatius [of Antioch]: "Who is the Godbearer?" the latter answered: "It is he who carries Christ in his heart."[4]

This concept of wanting to be good or wanting to become a saint is a desire that is not only legitimate but necessary. You cannot become what you do not desire to become. Your desire is the spring that releases the energy that causes all of the atoms of your being and subconscious to come into alignment with that desire. Through our desires we create ourselves. Like dropping coins into a wishing well or pond, we drop our desires into our subconscious. One by one, then, life takes us through experiences whereby these desires are fulfilled. Thus, when we desire to be one with God, our lives change radically because within us we have the propelling force of our desires bringing us into circumstances that will lead us to fulfill those desires.

Regarding the desire to be a saint and to be one with God, consider these words of Jesus: "Be ye therefore perfect, even as your Father which is in heaven is perfect."[5] With this statement, Jesus established the unalterable truth that the attainment of perfection is possible. I will explain. We understand that God is at once both perfect and transcendent, for he is continually transcending himself through his creation. So there is no ultimate in the cosmos, and yet God is and remains perfect.

Contrary to what we may think, perfection is also possible in this world, but it is not human perfection that we seek. Rather, our striving for internal perfection is fundamental to our spiritual path. For if we accept imperfection, or believe that we are perfect just the way we are, we eliminate the path of spiritual striving. And so the attainment of God-perfection is possible because perfection is the natural estate of man toward which the soul gravitates.

Thus, the desire to be perfect, the desire to be good, the desire to be a saint, a sage, or an adept is a legitimate desire. We need not feel guilty about this desire, although we may at times feel the condemnation or ridicule of the world. But in order to champion such desires, we will find ourselves coming apart from the mass consciousness.

The Mystical Path Today

Because the Church no longer teaches the path to union with God, God has come forward with another spiritual path so that all the truths the mystics have discovered in the different mystical traditions—all these rays from the sun returning to the Source—might quicken us and give to us an understanding that we can also follow back to the Source. This is the path we pursue and teach at Summit University,[6] our modern-day mystery school for those who desire to transcend themselves and reach the goal of union with God.

We who aspire to the mystical path today can call ourselves lightbearers. The Greek word *Christos* means "anointed"— anointed with the light. We are lightbearers because we have the presence of the light, the Christ, in our bodies and minds. Whether we feel it or not, this light inundates our soul, infiring our heart as though waves were breaking on the shore of our being. Because we have this inner light, we *are* that light and the light is us and we are transformed, even exalted, by it.

A *lightbearer*, then, is a "Christ-bearer." And when we feel the light, what we are feeling is our Higher Self, our Christ Self, occupying our souls and our body temples until the coming of our Sweet Jesus. As we nurture the flame of Christ in our hearts, we know a gentle oneness that gradually becomes a more powerful union.

The teaching that I bring to you is that God has placed within us a portion of himself, a tripartite flame that anchors his love, wisdom and power. Through this gift of the God flame, our soul has the potential to realize God consciousness, fulfill her reason for being on earth, and become one with God.

I give you this teaching because I have seen that as individuals experience the presence of that flame and yet are simultaneously dealing with their karma, they find it difficult to bear the juxtaposition of being one moment in God and the next moment feeling apart from God when they find themselves again dealing with the human condition.

Unless these individuals have wise spiritual counselors, they often do not understand that this process of soul purification is a part of the path that we all must go through before we unite ultimately with God. Teresa of Avila, reading the psalmist's description of his soul's anguish during those times when he was not in communion with his Lord, reflected, "It consoled me to know that other persons...had experienced so extreme a solitude."[7]

Teresa of Avila, John of the Cross, and other great luminaries have documented their experiences and their understanding of the mystical path. Their writings have provided consolation to many.

It is for this reason that we also offer books, lectures and courses—to offer hope and a path for souls passing through the labyrinth of their karma on their way to union with God. As we explore the mystical path in this book, I think you will recognize that you have walked some part of this path but perhaps did not understand it as such.

Mysticism as the Solution to Soul Agony

Many people living today find nothing in this world that really brings them any lasting joy. I believe that when people reach this state, it is because their soul is yearning for God but they do not have the spiritual tools or the teachings they need. Thus, they do not understand that everything in life is always planned by God to propel us to go inside and find the kingdom within and the Christ within.

When we look at our lives and our surroundings, we may at times consider that we have had problems, suffering and encounters that don't match up to what we would consider a part of the good life, the kind of happiness mankind generally seek. In these moments we miss the realization that our circumstances are gifts from a God who loves us, who chastens us, who allows our karma to descend because he sees that we are able to come to grips with it. And all of this is not to punish us or to create the hardened cynic, but to soften the heart, to mellow the heart in its love for God.

Thomas Merton, a twentieth-century writer, reflected, "The spiritual anguish of man has no cure but mysticism."[8] The mystical path is the solution to soul agony. It is a path that is known, a path that can be studied, learned and walked today. Knowing what other mystics have been through brings comfort and understanding to souls who are experiencing both the soul agony that accompanies facing the burdens of their karma and also the tremendous light of God that they feel in moments of communion with the Divine.

It is the Sacred Heart of Jesus in which, and upon which, the mystical path of Christianity rests. It is truly a path of profound love. This is what we will hear echoed to us as we listen with the heart to the teachings of the mystics who have outlined and clarified this path so that we, too, might walk it all the way Home. I pray that you will take this book as a meditation to feel the Presence of God and the fire of Christ in your heart.

PART ONE

The Indwelling Presence

CHAPTER 1

An Experience That Transforms the Soul

ysticism is not merely a belief or a philosophy; it is an experience that transforms the soul. If you aren't transformed, you haven't had the experience. When your soul is fully transformed, you and God are no longer two, but one. In the act of union with God, said the fourteenth-century mystic Johannes Tauler, there is "nothing in the soul beside God."[1] Saint Francis of Assisi so dedicated himself to the imitation of Christ that he was called "another Christ."

The fifteenth-century mystic Saint Catherine of Genoa experienced oneness as submersion in the ocean of God's love: "My being is God, not by simple participation but by a true transformation of my being.... I am so placed and submerged in His immense love, that I seem as though immersed in the sea, and nowhere able to touch, see or feel aught but water.... My Me is God, nor do I recognize any other Me except my God Himself."[2]

As we shall see, the mystical path is a spiritual journey into the heart of God's love. But the mystic knows that in order to be completely bonded to God's heart he must transcend the lesser self. Thus, the path of the mystic is a path of challenge as well as a path of joy. It is the challenge of working through the karma that gives you the sense of being separate from God and then the joy of going beyond that pain to the bliss of encountering your Lord face to face.

The Origins of Mysticism

The word *mysticism* is thought to be derived from the Greek word meaning "to close the eyes or lips." It was first used in connection with the Greek mystery religions. "Mystics" were those who promised to keep secret the rituals of their religion.

Neoplatonic philosophers who called their doctrines mystical taught their pupils to shut their eyes to the external world and go within, in profound contemplation, to discover mystical truths. I believe the reason they taught their pupils to close their eyes and go within was to develop their spiritual senses, including inner sight and hearing.

Closing their eyes meant they had to go to a plane of consciousness apart from the concrete mind. They had to go beyond the intellectual mind to levels of both the superconscious and the subconscious where the soul has direct awareness of her identity in God beyond the confines of the physical-intellectual self. The Neoplatonists sought to take their pupils to the compartment of being where the soul speaks to God and where God speaks to the soul.

Philo, a Jewish religious thinker and contemporary of Jesus, used "mystical" to refer not to secret rituals but to the hidden meaning of God's word. The early Greek Church Fathers Clement and Origen of Alexandria applied the word to the allegorical interpretation of scripture.

Origen believed there could be no real understanding of the

Origen of Alexandria

scriptures without communion with God. For Origen, interpretation of the scriptures was a religious experience. Thus he was the first to use "mystical" to describe a way of knowing God. Indeed, a number of the great themes within the genre of mystical literature go back to Origen.

In later centuries, Christians used the term *mystical* to indicate the hidden and sacred presence of Christ in the scriptures, sacraments and liturgy. The influential writings of the fifth- or sixth-century writer known as Pseudo-Dionysius established the word as part of the Christian vocabulary. He didn't just use it to discuss the interpretation of scripture; he also encouraged the exercise of "mystical contemplation," leaving behind "the senses and operations of the intellect"[3] in order to gain union with God. Eventually "mystical theology" was used in the Church to denote knowledge about God gained through contemplation.

Each Age Brings New Revelations of God

Those who long to know and see God are tapping into the soul's ever-present knowledge of the Higher Self and the higher calling. We sense ourselves to be extensions of God, and indeed we are souls and fiery spirits, spiritual beings, wearing garments of flesh like an overcoat we have put on in this life and many times before. Our soul predated this body and will exist after the physical form we wear no longer serves our soul's needs.

The creation of a new body, therefore, is not the creation of a new soul. Each time our soul prepares to reembody, she is filled with the sense of going back to pick up dropped stitches, finish her work and then give the world something of herself—an artistic creation, a gift of love and sweetness, kindness, or some great achievement.

Thus, although the outer mind may not have a clue, our soul knows at subconscious levels that she is meant to be reunited with her Lord. Lifetime after lifetime this soul-knowledge has impelled us to the feet of our teachers, some true, some false. We have drunk from the communion cups of the world's religions and have savored something of the Lord's essence from each one.

And so, in order to give his children a new awareness of himself, God releases new religions. We cannot assimilate God all at once. Just as we don't eat the food of a lifetime in a day, but portion by portion, so we assimilate God crumb by crumb.

During specific periods of time called ages, a civilization, a continent or an entire planet is destined to assimilate a certain attribute of God. The opening of these epochs is accompanied by the birth of an *avatar*, from the Sanskrit term meaning "incarnation of God." This avatar embodies the Word (the Christ) as it applies to the dispensation he inaugurates.

The length of an age, approximately 2,150 years, is related to the precession of the equinoxes. This is the astronomical term used to describe the slow movement of the earth's polar axis. As the axis moves, the point of the spring equinox moves through the signs of the zodiac, denoting which age we are in.

The equinox point takes about 2,150 years to go through 30 degrees of the zodiac, or one astrological sign. So, although no one knows exactly when each age begins or ends, we do know that about four thousand years ago we entered the age of Aries. About two thousand years ago we entered the age of Pisces. And today we are entering the age of Aquarius.

God as Father, Lawgiver and Universal Law

Each age marks a new dispensation of light from God that gives to earth's evolutions a new awareness of God's Presence. I see the dispensation of Aries as bringing the awareness of God as Father, Lawgiver and the embodiment of universal Law itself. This age was characterized by God's direct communion with Moses and God's gift to all generations of his name I AM THAT I AM,[4] whereby they, too, could commune with God. Moses showed us that it was the divine right of every son and daughter of God to walk and talk with the Indwelling Presence of God, the Great I AM. The condition: "Keep my commandments."[5]

Also in the Arian age and a century before Moses, the Egyptian pharaoh Ikhnaton introduced monotheism in Egypt and attained mystical union with God through his meditation on the sun and on the Sun behind the sun—the spiritual Cause behind the physical effect we see as our own sun and all other stars and star systems. Ikhnaton called God *Aton*. The symbol for Aton was the sun with diverging rays ending in hands. This symbolized that man is the hand of God in action and that as the sun and its rays are one, so there is no separation between Creator and creation. The name Ikhnaton means "he who serves the Aton." The pharaoh believed that he was a son of Aton. He truly knew himself as the light-emanation of the one God.

Moses and the Burning Bush

God as Son, Christ and Intercessor

The age of Pisces brought the awareness of God as the Son, revealed to us in the Universal Christ, the light-emanation, or "only begotten Son" of God, personified in the Christ Jesus. In Jesus the son of man was fully integrated with the Christ. Jesus came to show us the goal of our life—to fully merge with that Christ. He showed us how to walk the path of personal Christhood so that we too could realize the Son of God, the Christ, within ourselves. The condition: "Love me and keep my commandments."[6] The prophet Jeremiah prophesied the full revelation of the Son of God who should appear in the age of Pisces. He saw the Son as "The Lord Our Righteousness."[7]

God as Holy Spirit and Divine Mother

The dawning age of Aquarius brings us the awareness of God as the Holy Spirit and as the Divine Mother. In this age the divine Feminine is destined to be exalted in both male and female as the sacred fire that rises on the altar of our being. In this age our soul is destined to don the wedding garment for her fusion with the Divine Mother and the Holy Spirit. The condition we must fulfill is self-transcendence through divine love.

In summary, we can only see ourselves as we see God; there is no other model for our spiritual being. This is a fundamental principle of the path of mysticism. If we polish our soul and polish the mirror of the soul and direct that mirror through attention to God, then we will always be able to look in the mirror of our soul and see God. Thus, the unfoldment of God's identity within us and our identification with it will culminate in our direct experience of God followed by our union with God. This is the goal of all of our past incarnations and the goal of our life today.

Power through the Names of God

In each age God has also given us one or more new names whereby we may invoke that new image or attribute and, by reflection, make it our own. The names of God that come to us from the great religious traditions of the world are keys, each providing access to a portion of God's energy. As we pour devotion to God through a particular name, it's as if we now have a different-shaped cookie cutter to use when making cookies. Just as cookies will come out according to the shape we have chosen, so the light that pours to us through a particular name of God will carry the unique vibration of that name.

Over time we may develop the attunement to perceive the distinct and separate vibration of God that we are receiving through intoning a particular name. When God revealed the name I AM THAT I AM to Moses at Mount Sinai, he said, "This is my name forever, and this is my memorial unto all generations."[8] With the gift of this name, God revealed his Presence as individualized for each of us—our *personalized* I AM THAT I AM, a portion of his being and consciousness. Thus, each time we learn a new name by which to invoke God, we gain access to a portion of God's Self that was previously beyond our reach.

Knowledge of the names of God is empowerment. God has empowered his people through many ages, and by that empowerment we have learned to expand the light within our chakras—spiritual centers within our body temple that allow for the exchange of energy from the spiritual world to our world and anchor different facets of God's consciousness.[9] The names of God are precious keys to God's heart, mind and spirit, and to that state of consciousness we are destined to mirror and to become.

You may wish to keep a notebook in which you write down the names of God that you learn. Since these names were given during a particular dispensation and for a particular people, they will not do you much good if you do not understand their meaning, the tradition out of which they came, and the nature of devotion of the people who first used those names. But when you truly and profoundly understand a name and the facet of God that it is a key to, you will find that you can put on and become that facet of God.

Intercession of the Saints

Just as we access various attributes of God through the use of different names, so too we can access the attributes and intercession of the heavenly beings by calling to them. We assume that the names we use for the saints and heavenly beings are their true names, but actually they are keys with which we access the portion of their being that they can offer to us. The portion we receive depends on the Great Law. Thus, when we call to a heavenly being by that name, invoking their assistance with devotion and in the name of God, we receive from that being only the light and power of God for which that name is a chalice and no more, for we are not yet at the level where we can receive a greater portion.

Karma prevents us from seeing ourselves accurately, so we need a mentor who can help us to see and overcome our weak points, see and develop our strong points. Thus, I encourage students who desire union with God to study the lives of the great saints and mystics and to select as a spiritual mentor the one they need the most, the one they can love the most, the one they feel the most drawn to, for thereby they will grow the most.

To bond with your chosen spiritual mentor, pray to that one. Walk and talk with him or her throughout the day. In any given situation, ask yourself: What would he do? Implore your mentor to tutor your soul. Never stop knocking on his door. The great saints are in our midst, willing to help us to accelerate our soul mastery.

Thérèse of Lisieux clearly expressed this desire of the saints to help us. Shortly before her passing she said:

> I feel especially that my mission is about to begin, my mission of making God loved as I love Him, of giving my little way to souls. If God answers my desires, my heaven will be spent on earth until the end of the world. Yes, I want to spend my heaven in doing good on earth.[10]

Beginning soon after her death and continuing to this day, thousands upon thousands of accounts of healings, conversions and intercession have been attributed to Saint Thérèse. This beloved saint was canonized just twenty-eight years after her passing.

Heavenly Help for Today's Mystics

In order to recognize and follow in the footsteps of the mystics, we need to know what the life of a mystic looks like, how he talks and thinks, how he views himself in relation to God. We need examples to show us the way, and the best examples are those who have already become one with God—the ascended masters, those saints and adepts who have risen out of every culture and religion and made their way home to God. We refer to them as ascended masters because they accelerated in consciousness to become one with God. They realized that God was where they were, in them, and that they were his vessel.

They were not satisfied to be mere reflections of God. Rather, they strove to be God in manifestation in their fullness of portion. To this end, they balanced the love, wisdom and power of their threefold flame, the spark of the Divine in their heart. They mastered time and space and circumstance—that is, they fulfilled the purpose of their soul's journey on earth and balanced at least 51 percent of their karma. (By the grace of God, souls who ascend with a portion of their karma remaining are allowed to balance the remainder from the ascended state through service to earth and her evolutions.) There are other requirements for the ascension as well, but these are the main ones.

Thus, having fulfilled all the requirements of the Law, these masters ascended into the white light of the I AM THAT I AM, free from the rounds of karma and rebirth, and became forever one with their God Presence. You, too, as a son or daughter of God, are called to ascend back to God when you have fulfilled all the requirements for the ascension.

Christians refer to the ascension as "going to heaven" and Jesus is the most well-known ascended master. Others will be familiar to you as well, among them Saint Francis of Assisi, Saint Thérèse of Lisieux, and Saint Teresa of Avila. Most are unknown. In this book we will trace the trials and triumphs of both well-known and unsung Christian saints and mystics who, having sought and found union with the Presence of God, are now ascended masters.

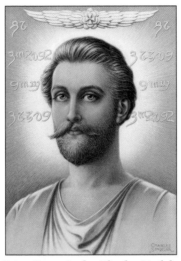

Saint Germain, by Charles Sindelar

Saint Germain: A Master for the Aquarian Age

Through these pages you will also come to know Saint Germain. I introduce him here because he plays a significant role in our lives in the age of Aquarius and because he is a prime example of an unsung ascended master. Over the course of many embodiments, during the last of which he was known throughout the courts of eighteenth-century Europe as the Comte de Saint Germain, he strove to bring the light of the Christ and the alchemy of freedom to the people of earth.

To give you a sense of the contributions that made this great adept an ascended master, I highlight here his embodiment in the thirteenth century as Roger Bacon, a keenly perceptive scientist, philosopher, monk, alchemist and prophet.

Bacon believed that he derived his awareness from "true knowledge," which, he said, "stems not from the authority of others, nor from a blind allegiance to antiquated dogmas." Two of his biographers write that he believed knowledge "is a highly personal

Detail, Statue of Roger Bacon, Oxford University Museum

experience—a light that is communicated only to the innermost privacy of the individual through the impartial channels of all knowledge and of all thought."[11]

And so Bacon, who had been a lecturer at Oxford and the University of Paris, separated himself from academe to seek and find his science in religion. Entering the Franciscan Order of Friars Minor, he said, "I will conduct my experiments on the magnetic forces of the lodestone at the selfsame shrine where my fellow-scientist, St. Francis, performed his experiments on the magnetic forces of love."[12]

But the friar's scientific and philosophical world view, his bold attacks on the theologians of his day, and his study of alchemy, astrology and magic led to his imprisonment by fellow Franciscans on charges of "heresies and novelties." He remained in solitary confinement for fourteen years and was released only shortly before his death. Although the clock of this life had run out and his body was broken, he knew that his efforts would not be without impact on the future.

Today, from the ascended state, Saint Germain is committed to helping us attain our eternal freedom. Due to his efforts on our behalf before the courts of heaven, some of the more arduous practices of the early Christian mystics, especially with regard to the balancing of karma, have been superseded by the spiritual teachings and practices he sponsors for our age.

The saints and ascended masters are our immortal teachers and we can learn from what they experienced when they were on earth. They are here today, seen and unseen, in our very midst. And they continue to teach us just as the adepts of ancient times imparted their teachings—heart-to-heart to a trusted inner circle of devotees.

Prayers and Meditations

The experience of God in the here and now is the grand adventure that the mystic pursues. To facilitate this experience , each chapter will conclude with a selection of spoken prayers and meditations. I invite you to use these as a profound meditation on God in order to cultivate, and perhaps to feel, his Presence as the fire of Christ within your heart.

Adoration to God

Give this prayer slowly and with devotion. Doing so helps you to feel closer to your God Presence, the I AM THAT I AM. Try giving it at the beginning of your prayer session. Then notice, as you go about your day, whether you feel more anchored in God and more at peace with your loved ones and others.

As you say the words, reflect on their meaning. Visualize yourself ascending in consciousness toward your God Presence. Feel the bliss of God. Imagine that you are surrounded by a suffusion of beautiful pink light. See the light penetrating every cell of your body. Sense and know that you are being transformed, particle by particle, as you experience oneness with God and with all creation.

> *Beloved mighty I AM Presence,*
> *Thou life that beats my heart,*
> *Come now and take dominion,*
> *Make me of thy life a part.*
> *Rule supreme and live forever*
> *In the flame ablaze within;*
> *Let me from thee never sever,*
> *Our reunion now begin.*

All the days proceed in order
From the current of thy power,
Flowing forward like a river,
Rising upward like a tower.
I AM faithful to thy love ray
Blazing forth light as a sun;
I AM grateful for thy right way
And thy precious word "Well done."

I AM, I AM, I AM adoring thee! (3 times)
O God, you are so magnificent! (9 times)
I AM, I AM, I AM adoring thee! (3 times)

Moving onward to perfection,
I AM raised by love's great grace
To thy center of direction—
Behold, at last I see thy face.
Image of immortal power,
Wisdom, love, and honor, too,
Flood my being now with glory,
Let my eyes see none but you!

O God, you are so magnificent! (3 times)
I AM, I AM, I AM adoring thee! (9 times)
O God, you are so magnificent! (3 times)

My very own beloved I AM!
Beloved I AM! Beloved I AM!

The Covenant of the Magi

Father, into thy hands I commend my being. Take me and use me—my efforts, my thoughts, my resources, all that I AM—in thy service to the world of men and to thy noble cosmic purposes, yet unknown to my mind.

Teach me to be kind in the way of the Law that awakens men and guides them to the shores of Reality, to the confluence of the River of Life, to the Edenic source, that I may understand that the leaves of the tree of life, given to me each day, are for the healing of the nations; that as I garner them into the treasury of being and offer the fruit of my loving adoration to thee and to thy purposes supreme, I shall indeed hold covenant with thee as my guide, my guardian, my friend.

For thou art the directing connector who shall establish my lifestream with those heavenly contacts, limited only by the flow of the hours, who will assist me to perform in the world of men the most meaningful aspect of my individual life plan as conceived by thee and executed in thy name by the Karmic Board of spiritual overseers who, under thy holy direction, do administer thy laws.

So be it, O eternal Father, and may the covenant of thy beloved Son, the living Christ, the Only Begotten of the Light, teach me to be aware that he liveth today within the tri-unity of my being as the Great Mediator between my individualized Divine Presence and my human self; that he raiseth me into Christ consciousness and thy divine realization in order that as the eternal Son becomes one with the Father, so I may ultimately become one with thee in that dynamic moment when out of union is born my perfect freedom to move, to think, to create, to design, to fulfill, to inhabit, to inherit, to dwell and to be wholly within the fullness of thy light.

Father, into thy hands I commend my being.

CHAPTER 2

God Dwells within You

he apostle Paul instructed the Corinthians, "Know ye not that ye are the temple of God, and that the Spirit of God dwelleth in you?"[1] How often do we think, as we walk about, that a mighty Spirit of God is dwelling in our body temple, living in us, and that God's Spirit is infiring us and impelling us to fulfill our mission and to love and comfort everyone we meet? The mystics believed that the soul is meant to be the dwelling place of God and a partaker of the divine nature. Their path of ascent to God included pursuit of the Indwelling Presence of God and of direct intercourse with God through prayer and contemplation.

In Christian mysticism this teaching goes back to the words of Jesus and the apostles. At the Last Supper Jesus promised his disciples, "If a man love me, he will keep my words: and my Father will love him, and we will come unto him, and make our abode with him."[2] Keeping in our heart the words of Jesus and ultimately the Word that he was, the I AM THAT I AM, makes us one with him. This is Jesus' promise: that the Father (the mighty Presence of the I AM) and the Son (the Christ) will take up their abode in our temple here and now, while we are in embodiment, if we keep Jesus' words, if we maintain the spirit of the living flame of love burning in our hearts, if we express the compassion of Christ to all.

This can happen to us more quickly than we realize when we determine no more to behave after the carnal mind but after the Christ. For as Paul wrote to the Romans: "To be carnally minded is death; but to be spiritually minded is life and peace.... For as many as are led by the Spirit of God, they are the sons of God.... The Spirit itself beareth witness with our spirit, that we are the children of God: And if children, then heirs; heirs of God, and joint-heirs with Christ.[3]

It is a wondrous thing to walk about in a vessel of clay and to realize that God inhabits this temple and that we have the power to increase and intensify his habitation by living a Spirit-filled life. Or we can diminish God's Presence in us to nothing by maintaining a state of anger, selfishness, sensuality, et cetera. We are the masters of our body temple. We decree whether God shall find room in us. Peter said that through the goodness and glory of Christ we can be "partakers of the divine nature"[4] here and now. Death is not a passport to this experience. I invite you, here and now, to partake of the divine nature.

A Divine Spark within Every Soul

Meister Eckhart taught:
There is something in the soul that is so akin to God that it is one with Him.... God's seed is within us.[5]... There is a part of the soul that is untouched by time or mortality; it proceeds out of the Spirit and remains eternally in the Spirit and is divine.... Here God glows and flames without ceasing, in all His abundance and sweetness and rapture.[6]

He could not have so written had he not so experienced. It is my hope that you, too, will experience again and again the fire of God that "glows and flames without ceasing" in your heart. During moments of prayer and meditation, put your hand over your heart and lovingly caress your heart. I pray that you will feel the Presence of God as the fire of Christ in your heart.

Meister Eckhart also wrote, "The spark of the soul...is created by God.... [It] is a light imprinted from above.... [It] is an image of the divine nature, which always opposes what is not divine. It is...always inclined to the good."[7] He taught: "Since God Himself has sown this seed [of God within us], impressed and impregnated it, it can indeed be covered over and hidden, but never destroyed or extinguished in itself; it glows and gleams, shines and burns and inclines without ceasing towards God."[8]

Christ Is Formed in You

In addition to their belief that all men are by nature like God and that within every soul there is a spark of the Divine, the early mystics believed that the Indwelling Christ is formed within the individual. Paul was the first to record this concept. He wrote, "I live; yet not I, but Christ liveth in me."[9] Paul discovered not only that Christ lived in him but that when Christ lived in him, he no longer lived in himself. Thus, he no longer perceived himself to be simply Paul; rather he was Paul, one with the Christ.

Paul also proclaimed the Indwelling Christ as the inheritance of all Christians. He wrote to the Galatians, "I travail in birth again until Christ be formed in you."[10] He told the Colossians that God would make known to his saints how great are "the riches of the glory of this mystery...which is Christ in you, the hope of glory."[11] The manner in which Christ is formed in us is that we allow it. To prepare ourselves to receive him, we can give attention daily to

The Ecstasy of Saint Paul, *by Nicolas Poussin*

Jesus Christ, to the Indwelling Christ, and to the flame of Christ within our heart.

Origen wrote: "Not just in Mary did [Christ's] birth begin ... but in you, too, if you are worthy, is the WORD of God born. If you are so pure in mind, so holy in body and so blameless in deed, you can give birth to Christ himself."[12] Is it any wonder that Origen's words were anathematized? To state in the third or fourth century that we, too, can give birth to Christ was considered blasphemy. Meister Eckhart taught that the birth of the Son of God within the individual is even more important than the incarnation of the historical Jesus. He reasoned, "It is more worthy of God that He should be born spiritually...of every good soul, than that He should have been born physically of Mary."[13] These are dramatic statements for those times.

Author Sidney Spencer explains that for some mystics, Christ is

not merely a historical person, but a universal principle—the Word, the Logos, the Son of God, the divine Light in men.... This "divine humanity" is incarnate wherever men rise into union with God. It is natural therefore that [the mystics] should speak of the birth of the spiritual consciousness in man as the birth of Christ in him. The Quakers [for example] use the term "Light of Christ" interchangeably with "the Inner Light."[14]

For the eighteenth-century Protestant mystic William Law, Christ is "the Son or Word of God incarnate in Jesus, but manifested also wherever men turn to God in faith and love." Law believed that Christ is "a universal principle, 'the life and light and holiness of every creature that is holy.' And it is the uprising of that principle within us which is 'the birth of Christ' in our souls."[15]

Paul also knew the Holy Spirit as an indwelling intercessor. He wrote:

> The Spirit also helpeth our infirmities: for we know not what we should pray for as we ought: but the Spirit itself maketh intercession for us with groanings which cannot be uttered. And he that searcheth the hearts knoweth what is the mind of the Spirit, because he maketh intercession for the saints according to the will of God.[16]

Paul is saying that he heard the voice of the Holy Spirit from within, offering prayers and supplications on behalf of his soul with groanings. Think how the Spirit of God strives to bring us back to the place of our soul's oneness with God! Paul is also saying that the Indwelling Christ of each one knows the mind of the Holy Spirit because the Spirit intercedes in our behalf according to God's will. So we can call to the Holy Spirit and ask him to intercede for us in all matters that burden us.

The birth of Christ in our consciousness and in our souls comes when we have companionship with the Christ Presence.

This new birth of consciousness is a certain awakening within us of a larger sphere of selfhood that we have yet to fill in; and we accomplish this by the intercession of the Holy Spirit. The babe must grow and wax strong in the spirit of the LORD until he comes to the full stature of his Sonship, his Christhood in God. When that takes place the soul is fused, or bonded, to Christ—to Jesus Christ and, through him, to the Indwelling Christ.

The Threefold Flame of the Trinity

What Meister Eckhart was describing as "the spark of the soul" is the *divine spark*, which is technically not a part of the soul. At times the mystics did not distinguish between the soul and the divine spark. The ascended masters teach that the seed of the Inner Christ is literally a spark of sacred fire from God's own heart. It is your soul's point of contact with the Supreme Source of all life. The soul is the potential of the individual to realize God. The divine spark is the means to its realization. Without the divine spark, the soul could not exercise her potential to realize God.

Saint Germain teaches that the Indwelling Presence of God is a threefold flame anchored in a secret chamber within the heart. This flame has three "plumes" that correspond to the Trinity of Father, Son and Holy Spirit and embody the three primary attributes of God—power, wisdom and love. So long as we tend this flame we have a unique identity in God and are forever tied to his heart. The ultimate, everlasting forgiveness of God should be known by us in this very gift of the threefold flame—our soul's potential to realize the allness of God as the allness of Self.

The goal of not one but many incarnations is to so fan the threefold flame with our devotion to God that it increases to the fullness of the Godhead dwelling in us bodily as it did in Jesus Christ. Jesus is our Lord and Saviour because the fullness of the

The Threefold Flame

Godhead dwelt in him bodily. Through him we may have that flame reignited if we have extinguished it through extreme violations of God's laws. Through him we may be bonded anew to our Holy Christ Self. Jesus has saved us for the opportunity to become immortal by taking upon himself our karma in the Piscean age. Jesus was and is the Word incarnate. He is the supreme mystic who lights the way for all who would follow his light to the fullness of God's light in themselves.

Your Divine Identity

Saint Germain opened the path of mysticism to the world in the twentieth century when he unveiled the Chart of Your Divine Self depicting your soul's mystical union with God. This Chart is an outline of your spiritual anatomy, a diagram of you and your potential to become who you really are. And it is a sign from the heart of Saint Germain to the mystics of all past ages who would reincarnate in this age that the hour for the fulfillment of your reason for being—union with God—has come. Through meditation on the Chart of Your Divine Self and a profound adoration of your God Presence, you will come closer to seeing the Holy of holies of your own God Reality.

The three figures in the Chart of Your Divine Self correspond to the Christian Trinity: The upper figure corresponds to the Father (who is one with the Mother), the middle figure to the Son, and the lower figure to the temple of the Holy Spirit.

We address our Father-Mother God as the I AM Presence. This is the I AM THAT I AM, the Lawgiver, whom God revealed to Moses and individualized for every son and daughter of God. Your I AM Presence is surrounded by seven concentric spheres of rainbow light. These make up your Causal Body, the biding place of your I AM Presence.

The spheres of your Causal Body are successive planes of God's consciousness that make up your heaven-world. They are the "many mansions" of our Father's house, where you lay up your "treasures in heaven." Your treasures are your words and works worthy of your Creator, constructive thoughts and feelings, your victories for the right, and the virtues you have embodied to the glory of God. When you judiciously exercise your free will to daily use the energies of God in love and in harmony, these energies automatically ascend to your Causal Body. They accrue to your soul as "talents" which you may then multiply as you put them to good use lifetime after lifetime.

The unveiling of the I AM THAT I AM as the individual I AM Presence of every child of God is the equivalent of the veil in the temple being rent in twain. The Old Testament speaks of the veil that divided the holy place into which the priests entered from the

The Chart of Your Divine Self—A Visualization for Mystical Union

Holy of holies, in which the ark of the covenant resided and into which the high priest alone entered once a year on the day of atonement.[17] The New Testament tells of the rending of that veil at the hour of Jesus' crucifixion.[18] The rending of the veil signified that thereafter all who accepted Jesus as the High Priest and Mediator in their lives would also have access to the individualized Christ, whom you appropriately address as your Holy Christ Self. Jesus reconnects the soul to her Holy Christ Self. We must have Jesus, our Lord and Saviour and Intercessor, for God has sent him for this very purpose that we might be saved.

The middle figure in the Chart of Your Divine Self represents the "only begotten Son" of the Father-Mother God, the Universal Christ. He is your personal mediator and your soul's advocate before God. John spoke of this individualized presence of the Son of God as "the true Light, which lighteth every man that cometh into the world."[19] He is your Higher Self, Inner Teacher, Divine Spouse, and dearest Friend, and he is most often recognized as the Guardian Angel. Your Holy Christ Self overshadows you every hour of the day and night. Draw nigh to him and he will draw nigh to you.

The lower figure in the Chart of Your Divine Self represents you as a disciple on the path of reunion with God. It is your soul evolving through the planes of Matter using the vehicles of the four lower bodies to balance karma and fulfill her divine plan. The four lower bodies are the etheric body (memory body); the mental body; the desire body (emotional body); and the physical body.

The lower figure is surrounded by a tube of light, which is projected from the heart of the I AM Presence in answer to your call. It is a cylinder of white light that sustains a forcefield of protection twenty-four hours a day, so long as you maintain your harmony in thought, feeling, word and deed. (See pages 75 and 161 for how to invoke this protective tube of light.)

Sealed in the secret chamber of your heart is the threefold flame of Life. It is your divine spark, the gift of life, consciousness and free will from your beloved I AM Presence. Through the love, wisdom and power of the Godhead anchored in your threefold flame, your soul can fulfill her reason for being on earth. Also called the Christ flame and the liberty flame, or fleur-de-lis, the threefold flame is the spark of the soul's Divinity, her potential for Christhood.

The silver (or crystal) cord is the stream of life, or "lifestream," which descends from the heart of the I AM Presence through the Holy Christ Self to nourish and sustain (through the seven chakras and the secret chamber of the heart) the soul and her four lower bodies. It is over this 'umbilical' cord that the light of the Presence flows, entering the being of man at the crown chakra and giving impetus for the pulsation of the threefold flame in the secret chamber of the heart.

The lower figure represents the son of man or child of the light evolving beneath his own 'Tree of Life'. The lower figure corresponds to the Holy Spirit, for the soul and the four lower bodies are intended to be the temple of the Holy Spirit. The violet flame, the spiritual fire of the Holy Spirit, envelops the soul as it purifies, and this is how you visualize yourself standing in the violet flame. You can invoke the violet flame daily in the name of your I AM Presence and Holy Christ Self to purify your four lower bodies and consume negative thoughts, negative feelings and negative karma in preparation for the ritual of the alchemical marriage—your soul's union, or spiritual marriage, with her Beloved, your Holy Christ Self, and with Christ Jesus.

Shown just above the head of the Christ is the dove of the Holy Spirit descending in the benediction of the Father-Mother God. When your soul has achieved the alchemical marriage, she is ready for the baptism of the Holy Spirit. At that time she may hear the

Father-Mother God pronounce the divine approbation, "This is my beloved Son, in whom I AM well pleased."

When your soul concludes a lifetime on earth, the I AM Presence withdraws the silver cord, whereupon your threefold flame returns to the heart of your Holy Christ Self. Your soul, clothed in her etheric garment, gravitates to the highest level of consciousness to which she has attained in all of her past incarnations. Between embodiments she is schooled in spiritual retreats located in the etheric plane (the heaven-world) until her final incarnation, when the Great Law decrees she shall return to the Great God Source to go out no more.

Your soul is the nonpermanent aspect of your being, which you make permanent through the ascension process. By this process your soul balances karma, bonds to your Holy Christ Self, fulfills her divine plan and returns at last to the living Presence of the I AM THAT I AM. Thus the cycles of her going out into the Matter cosmos are completed. In attaining union with God she has become the Incorruptible One, a permanent atom in the Body of God. The Chart of Your Divine Self is therefore a diagram of yourself—past, present and future.

Prayers and Meditations

The mystery of Christ's dwelling within us and yet needing to be formed in us is this: Until we are bonded, or fused, with Christ, Christ remains above us in higher planes of consciousness. Use the following visualization and prayers as meditations to accelerate your bonding.

Visualization for the Forming of Christ in You

Visualize the forming of Christ within you by imagining points of light coming together in concentration, at first dispersed and vapory with no form or shape. As you begin to know who and what Christ is and what are his attributes, works and words, there is forming within you your concept, or image, of that Christ whom you adore and worship, that Christ who is your brother, teacher and friend.

Christ is being formed in you each day, becoming more concentrated as light until his very Presence and outline and form are duplicated here below as the Indwelling Christ.

Try this visualization upon awakening or before retiring at night. As you visualize Christ being formed in you, place your hand over your heart and pour forth your devotion to the flame of Christ residing therein.

Holy Christ Flame

Thou Holy Christ Flame within my heart
Help me to manifest all thou art
Teach me to see thyself in all
Help me to show men how to call
All of thy glory from the Sun
'Til earth's great victory is won
I AM we love thee, thou art our all!
I AM we love thee, hear our call!

I hear thy call, my children dear
I AM thy heart, so never fear
I AM your mind, your body, too
I AM in every cell of you.
I AM thy earth and sea and sky
And not one soul shall I pass by
I AM in thee, thou art in me
I AM, I AM thy victory.

Introit to the Holy Christ Self

1. *Holy Christ Self above me,*
   Thou balance of my soul,
   Let thy blessed radiance
   Descend and make me whole.

Refrain:
   Thy flame within me ever blazes,
   Thy peace about me ever raises,
   Thy love protects and holds me,
   Thy dazzling light enfolds me.
   I AM thy threefold radiance,
   I AM thy living Presence
   Expanding, expanding, expanding now.

2. *Holy Christ Flame within me,*
   Come, expand thy triune light;
   Flood my being with the essence
   Of the pink, blue, gold and white.

3. *Holy lifeline to my Presence,*
   Friend and brother ever dear,
   Let me keep thy holy vigil,
   Be thyself in action here.

CHAPTER 3

The Rebirth of the Mystical Path

Two thousand years ago, the apostle Paul announced the opening of the sealed treasury of sacred mysteries. But, as Paul said, this was the wisdom of Christ for those who could receive the Christic experience. It was to be spoken only "among them that are perfect." Paul's words are at the heart of Christian mysticism as embodied by Jesus Christ. They go to the heart of that *gnosis* (self-knowledge) taught by Jesus to his disciples. They go to the very root of Christian mysticism.

In his First Epistle to the Corinthians, Paul wrote:

We speak wisdom among them that are perfect: yet not the wisdom of this world, nor of the princes of this world [that is, the fallen angels] that come to nought:

But we speak the wisdom of God in a mystery, even the hidden wisdom, which God ordained before the world unto our glory....

But as it is written, Eye hath not seen, nor ear heard, neither have entered into the heart of man, the things which God hath prepared for them that love him.

But God hath revealed them unto us by his Spirit: for the Spirit searcheth all things, yea, the deep things of God....

For who hath known the mind of the Lord, that he may instruct him? But we have the mind of Christ.[1]

Through the centuries and ages we have embodied time and time again, and in each lifetime we have expanded and deepened our understanding of God and our true nature. And at a precise moment in cosmic history (1875, as near as I can determine) we experienced a cosmic rebirth. In that year, under a new dispensation, the ascended masters opened that same sealed treasury of hidden mysteries and began delivering the wisdom of God through a number of contacts and amanuenses, including mystics who had been their pupils for centuries, notably throughout the Piscean, or Christian, dispensation.

An Everlasting Covenant

Through the Theosophical Society, the world of metaphysics, the I AM movement, the Agni Yoga Society, and then The Summit Lighthouse, they delivered "the deep things of God" to all who would accept them. Thus, in the Aquarian age, the dispensation proclaimed by Paul for the elect—speaking the wisdom of God in a mystery—is replaced by that which was prophesied during the age of Aries by Isaiah.

Isaiah foretold for our time and age the opportunity for salvation to all who would drink at the fount of the waters of everlasting life—all who would drink, not just those who were ready for the Christ experience, not just them that were perfect, not just the inner circle.

These words of Isaiah I have cherished since my earliest

Detail, Isaiah's Lips Anointed with Fire, *by Benjamin West*

childhood readings of the Bible. It's likely that you are familiar with them, but perhaps you didn't know that Isaiah's prophecy was the unfurling of the future dispensation for our time. Isaiah was very powerful. You can imagine how he delivered this in the marketplace:

> Ho, every one that thirsteth, come ye to the waters, and he that hath no money; come ye, buy, and eat; yea, come, buy wine and milk without money and without price.

Imagine this glorious opening and freedom. Isaiah is saying the teachings are free and freely given.

> Wherefore do ye spend money for that which is not bread? And your labour for that which satisfieth not?... Incline your ear [to God] and come unto me: hear, and your soul shall live; and I will make an everlasting covenant with you.

Listen with your inner ear, for God is making a contract. He's drawing up a contract with you, his sons and daughters, and it's an everlasting, unending contract.

> Seek ye the LORD while he may be found, call ye upon him while he is near.

Isaiah is speaking of the dispensations of those ages in which God draws nigh to the people through the avatars and the saints. But then centuries go by, dark ages, in which there is no spark of light or enlightenment. So while God is nigh, draw nigh to him. Pursue him with the white-hot heat of your spirit.

Then Isaiah speaks to the wicked and to those who have sinned, who perhaps think they cannot come near the prophet who is the voice of God speaking in the square. And so he says:

> Let the wicked forsake his way, and the unrighteous man his thoughts: and let him return unto the LORD [the mighty I AM Presence], and he will have mercy upon him; and to our God, for he will abundantly pardon.

This is the mighty dispensation initiated by Jesus Christ, the dispensation of forgiveness by the power of the Son of God. And it's the dispensation of Aquarius and the prophecy of the violet flame. Isaiah is saying: Turn your back on evildoings and face the Sun of your I AM Presence. Walk toward that Sun and never look back. Confess your sins, receive a penance. Get locked into God. Let your soul return to your mighty I AM Presence through your Holy Christ Self. Isaiah continues:

> For my thoughts are not your thoughts, neither are your ways my ways, saith the LORD.

This means: Abandon double-mindedness! God is single-minded. Let your eye be single. This is the message of Isaiah for today. It's the path taught by the ascended masters. And it's the message for our return to the Godhead. And then he seals it:

> So shall my word be that goeth forth out of my mouth: it shall not return unto me void.

And all the words that have ever been spoken by the prophets and messengers, the avatars and the Christs of all ages are going to the farthest ends of the universe. And they will not return unto God void! I see the Word going to the farthest expanses of cosmos, reaching that edge and then traveling all the way back again into our hearts.

> It shall not return unto me void, but it shall accomplish that which I please, and it shall prosper in the thing whereto I sent it.

In this prophecy spoken through Isaiah, God is foretelling the day when we, as God's instruments, will exercise the power of his spoken Word. This is why the ascended masters have given us prayers to use. Because they have attained union with God, the prayers they give us come from God, they are the words of God. Thus, when we say those words, our decree—the Word that we send forth—will not return unto us void unless we set up a blockade and don't allow it to return. That is the power of the spoken Word. This is why our prayers are called decrees, and every one of us can exercise this power.

This is the promise spoken by Isaiah:

> For ye shall go out with joy, and be led forth with peace: the mountains and the hills shall break forth before you...singing, and all the trees of the field shall clap their hands.

What is this prophecy? That all of nature and the angelic hosts will serve you. The son, the daughter of God that serves the light and does so day after day, steadfastly, will wake up one day and find that the light serves him.

> Instead of the thorn shall come up the fir tree, and instead of the brier shall come up the myrtle tree.

Have you noticed the "thorn" and the "brier" growing in your backyard? Why are they there? They're negative karma. Isaiah is prophesying: Instead of reaping your negative karma you shall be in the joy of the violet flame (which transmutes karma by transforming the negative energy into positive energy) and you shall reap the rewards of your own righteousness and God's righteousness through you.

> And it shall be to the LORD for a name, for an everlasting sign that shall not be cut off.[2]

This dispensation, delivered to us through the teachings of the ascended masters, will not be cut off. God will not cut it off. The only person that can cut off this dispensation is you.

These two dispensations are at hand today. The former, articulated by Paul "for them that are perfect," is now open to "every one that thirsteth" because of the sponsorship of Jesus Christ and the ascended masters. And the latter dispensation, which was thundered by Isaiah for Aquarius, is for all who will freely drink of the waters.

Prayers and Meditations

Prayer for Attunement

In this prayer, you are inviting God to act on your behalf. Try giving it in the morning as you begin your day. Consciously surrender your problems to your mighty I AM Presence and Holy Christ Self, and then observe how the tenor of your day improves.

Beloved mighty I AM Presence,
   Father of all Life—
Act on my behalf this day:
   Fill my form.
Release the light that is necessary
   For me to go forth to do thy will,
And see that at every hand the decisions I make
   Are according to thy holy will.
See that my energies are used to magnify
   The Lord in everyone whom I meet.
See to it that thy holy wisdom released to me
   Is used constructively for the expansion
   of God's kingdom.
And above all, beloved heavenly Father,
   I commend my spirit unto thee
And I ask that as thy flame is one with my flame,
   The union of these two flames shall pulsate
To effect in my world
   The continuous alertness and attunement
Which I need with thy holy Presence,
   With the Holy Spirit, and with the World Mother.

Salutation to the Sun

This powerful prayer sets your course toward oneness with your God Presence. It helps you to manifest outwardly the divinity that is within. Repeat the decree slowly at first, then more quickly as you get to know the words. Eventually you can reach the state in which your mind has become one with the prayer and repeats it inwardly in unceasing communion with God, even while you attend to your daily responsibilities.

As you give this decree, visualize God's light descending into your body temple and expanding from your heart to create a large spherical ovoid of light that extends three feet from your body in all directions.

O mighty Presence of God, I AM,
in and behind the Sun:
I welcome thy light, which floods all the earth,
into my life, into my mind,
into my spirit, into my soul.
Radiate and blaze forth thy light!
Break the bonds of darkness and superstition!
Charge me with the great clearness
of thy white fire radiance!
I AM thy child, and each day I shall become
more of thy manifestation!

CHAPTER 4

Mystical Contemplation and Prayer

orollary to the mystics' belief in the Indwelling Presence of God is their premise that the soul can have direct intercourse with God through mystical contemplation and prayer. I refer to mystical contemplation as meditation. Through meditation we seek to still the outer self in order to enter a state of listening grace, in which our inner ears and eyes are fixed on our I AM Presence and Holy Christ Self. Meditation does not involve effort or strain. Rather, it is a practice of gentle submission to knowing and becoming God's will and wisdom and love. In this state we become receptive to God's virtues and unfailing guidance.

Communion with God through prayer occurs in two essential forms: devotional prayer and invocative prayer. In devotional prayer we give our all to God—our whole heart and soul and mind and love. Invocative prayer is the form we use to call forth the allness of God and his love— to invoke his heart and soul and mind to enter our being.

To the early mystics, prayer was not just the repetition of a prescribed set of devotions and petitions to God, and neither can it be rote repetition for us today. True prayer, whether silent or spoken, is an interior prayer wherein we speak with God from the very depths of our soul. It is a form of concentration upon God. It is a profound and unceasing communion, free from distractions within and distractions without, that sets our soul on fire.

Saint John Climacus, the seventh-century abbot of a monastery on Mount Sinai, wrote: "Prayer is by nature a dialog and a union of man with God. Its effect is to hold the world together."[1] I would add that everyone who maintains this kind of relationship with God is holding the Spirit cosmos and the Matter cosmos together, because in that dialogue and union he comes to the level of consciousness of the Son of God, the Holy Christ Self.

An Intimate Sharing between Friends

Saint Thérèse of Lisieux, who lived in the nineteenth century, described her simple manner of praying and sharing with God:

> With me prayer is a lifting of the heart; a glance towards Heaven; a cry of gratitude and love, uttered equally in sorrow and in joy. In a word, it is something noble, supernatural, which expands my soul and unites it to God.... Apart from the Divine Office, which in spite of my unworthiness is a daily joy, I [do not] look through books for beautiful prayers.... I do as children who have not learnt to read—I simply tell Our Lord all that I want, and He always understands.[2]

Many people on earth are suffering and yet they do not pray or perhaps they do not know how to pray. For some the pain is so great that they cannot articulate it—feelings of frustration, anger, self-pity, aloneness and so many hurts and disappointments. Many feel that there is no longer any real depth or capacity for intimacy

Saint Thérèse of Lisieux

in spiritual matters or with another heart. And so the angels listen not only to prayers that are clearly formed but also to the unspoken expressions of the soul, for these, too, are a form of prayer.

In the 1500s Francisco de Osuna, a Franciscan friar, wrote a series of maxims urging the path of recollection as a means to union with God. Simply stated, in the practice of recollection the attention is placed on the presence of God in the soul. Osuna's Third Spiritual Alphabet, long considered to be a masterpiece of mystical literature, offers maxims for the practice of true interior prayer. In it he explained that those who wish to undertake any spiritual exercise must first understand that "friendship and communion with God are possible in this life of exile."[3]

Teresa of Avila, who used Osuna's *Third Spiritual Alphabet* as a guide to contemplation, further developed the theme of friendship with God through prayer. "Mental prayer," she wrote, "is nothing else than an intimate sharing between friends; it means taking time frequently to be alone with Him who we know loves us."[4] Just as "family ties and friendship are lost through a lack of communication,"[5] she said, so is our relationship with God lost if we don't pray.

We can set our mind and heart to anything. We are not the victim of our preferences; we create our preferences and we decide what to do with our hours. Think of how much time we spend doing so many things that really don't count—for instance, shopping or seeking entertainment. We celebrate, have feasts and parties, do this and that. Hours and hours may go by and we think nothing of it. But when it comes to kneeling or sitting in prayer, how long are we good for? How much patience do we have? And yet the quality of that experience is going to determine where our soul goes when the body is no longer capable of housing it. That's something to think about.

The third-century Neoplatonic philosopher Plotinus wrote, "We must be deaf to the sounds of the sense[s] and keep the soul's faculty of apprehension one-pointed and ready to catch visions

Saint Catherine's Monastery, Mount Sinai. Many mystics have sought a life free from worldly distractions in order to focus their attention on God.

from on high."⁶ To catch these visions we may have to remove ourselves from people, places and circumstances that are not conducive to our ongoing communion with God.

There are times when we simply have to be alone. The voice of our Christ Self and I AM Presence are quietly powerful while the voices of the world are raucously louder. So let's ask ourselves: Are the places we go and the things we do and the kind of TV we watch and the books we read really helping us to contact God and discover our Real Self? It's time that we look at the sands in the hourglass and take stock.

Sometimes, even when we are in church, distractions can present a challenge. An incident in the life of Thérèse of Lisieux shows her ingenuity in overcoming such a distraction. While she and the other sisters were in meditation in the choir, one of the sisters continually fidgeted with her rosary. The noise so distressed and irritated Thérèse that she began perspiring. At last, she wrote, "instead of trying not to hear it, which was impossible, I set myself to listen, as though it had been some delightful music, and my meditation—which was not the 'prayer of quiet'—was passed in offering this music to Our Lord."⁷

God Wants All of You

The mystics spoke of prayer as a profound experience. Walter Hilton, a fourteenth-century mystic, advised, "You should always seek with great diligence to come to the spiritual experience of God in prayer."⁸ Pray again and again until you have that experience. Cultivate ardor in prayer. One way to do this is to think of the thing you most like to do of all the things you do. Lock in that feeling, then transfer that ardor to prayer and see how your ardor in prayer will work for you.

John Climacus taught:

> Some emerge from prayer as from a blazing furnace and as though having been relieved of all material defilements. Others come forth as if they were resplendent with light and clothed in a garment of joy and of humility. But as for those who emerge without having experienced either of these effects, I would say that they have prayed in a bodily...manner, and not spiritually.[9]

In moments of profound prayer and giving decrees, you have the sublime opportunity of merging with your Holy Christ Self, of actually experiencing your own Christhood, whereas in the normal course of daily events you may not feel that as fully. You also have an opportunity to gain in your ability to release sacred fire through your energy centers.

I would counsel you to put forth the energy and the effort to endow your words with fire. Produce the fire here below so that your whole body can "ignite" and become the great conflagration of the I AM Presence above. Get into the driver's seat and at the same time know that the charioteer of your life is your Holy Christ Self.

One day you will stand alone before your God and the only thing that will count is the sacred fire you have externalized. If that is enough, you will be assumed unto God in the ritual of the ascension. If it is not, you will return to embodiment until you get that fire. So work while you have the light and strive for it. Give the best of your heart and energy and strength to get to the place where God can infill you.

Give God all you've got and he'll have something to use for this alchemy. Shake the very rafters of heaven with your prayers until the angels come very close and all the children of the light are finally and at last set free on this planet. Offer your prayers and decrees in the full God-authority of your living I AM Presence.

Angela of Foligno, a thirteenth-century Franciscan mystic, said that prayer will bring enlightenment, joy and ardent love if we give our all to it. She wrote:

> Prayer demands the entire man and not merely a part of him. It claims the whole heart and, if only a portion is given, a man achieves nothing.... Empty yourself; let [God] take over all of you, and He will give you a great light which will enable you to see yourself and see Him.[10]

Why is giving part of ourselves to God not enough? Because giving only part of ourselves to God is a violation of the first commandment, "Thou shalt have no other gods before me.... For I, the LORD thy God, am a jealous God."[11] God wants all of you because you are himself and he will not take just a part of you.

That doesn't mean that when you give all of yourself to God you will have nothing left for yourself. On the contrary, you will have yourself and God to do all the other lawful things you want to do. This is not a mournful path. This is a joyous path, a path that is simply God-filled.

Secret Exchanges between God and the Soul

Teresa of Avila, in her best-known work, *The Interior Castle*, described successive levels of the soul's communion with God. She compared the soul to "a castle made entirely out of a diamond or of very clear crystal, in which there are many rooms."[12]

Teresa described seven dwelling places in the castle and said that the closer the soul dwells to the center, the more light she receives. You can think of these seven places as the seven levels of spiritual awareness associated with the chakras, or the seven spheres of the Great Causal Body. They are represented in the Chart of Your Divine Self (opposite page 34) by the color bands surrounding the I AM Presence.

Teresa also discussed the obstacles to the soul's progress as well as what the soul can experience at each level. Some souls, she said, stay in the outer courtyard and don't even care about entering the castle. Others are able to penetrate to the center, the seventh dwelling place, "where God himself is." Here, she said, "the very secret exchanges between God and the soul take place" and the soul is finally united with her Lord.[13] Teresa's vision sounds so like the representation of the Great Causal Body in the Chart of Your Divine Self, with God, the mighty I AM Presence, in the center.

The door of entry to the interior castle, Teresa explained, is prayer and reflection, and she warned of the dangers of rote prayer:

> Vocal prayer...must be accompanied by reflection. A prayer in which a person is not aware of whom he is speaking to, what he is asking, who it is who is asking and of whom, I do not call prayer however much the lips move.... Anyone who has the habit of speaking before God's majesty as though he were speaking to a slave,...saying whatever comes to his head and whatever he has learned from saying at other times, in my opinion is not praying.[14]

We know all these things, yet how often do we think on these things? Prayers, mantras, affirmations and decrees don't work by themselves. It is our working of them, filling the words with light, endowing them with sacred fire, that makes them effective.

Union with God through the Word

Saint Germain speaks of going within the interior castle to the secret chamber of the heart. He teaches us to place our attention upon the heart as a means to strengthen our contact with the Divine:

> Your heart is indeed one of the choicest gifts of God. Within it there is a central chamber surrounded by...such light and protec-

tion that we call it a 'cosmic interval.' It is a chamber separated from Matter, and no probing could ever discover it. It occupies simultaneously not only the third and fourth dimensions but also other dimensions unknown to man.... [It] is thus the connecting point of the mighty silver cord of light that descends from your God Presence to sustain the beating of your physical heart, giving you life, purpose and cosmic integration.

I urge all men to treasure this point of contact that they have with Life by giving conscious recognition to it. You do not need to understand by sophisticated language or scientific postulation the how, why and wherefore of this activity. Be content to know that God is there and that within you there is a point of contact with the Divine, a spark of fire from the Creator's own heart [which is] called the threefold flame of Life. There it burns as the triune essence of love, wisdom and power.

Each acknowledgment paid daily to the flame within your heart will amplify the power and illumination of love within your being. Each such attention will produce a new sense of dimension for you, if not outwardly apparent then subconsciously manifest within the folds of your inner thoughts.

Neglect not, then, your heart as the altar of God. Neglect it not as the sun of your manifest being. Draw from God the power of love and amplify it within your heart. Then send it out into the world at large as the bulwark of that which shall overcome the darkness of the planet, saying:

> *I AM the light of the heart*
> *Shining in the darkness of being*
> *And changing all into the golden treasury*
> *Of the Mind of Christ.*
>
> *I AM projecting my love*
> *Out into the world*

To erase all errors
And to break down all barriers.

I AM the power of infinite love,
Amplifying itself
Until it is victorious,
World without end![15]

Saint Germain is the great adept who has made the mystical path available to all who will apply themselves. He did this by teaching us the path of devotion through the Science of the Spoken Word. When we say the prayer "I AM the Light of the Heart," we

Notre Dame de Paris. The architecture of the gothic cathedrals was inspired by the inner geometry of the secret chamber of the heart, where you commune with God and your Holy Christ Self.

are celebrating God where we are. In the very moment of reciting a prayer given to us by an ascended master, we are attaining union with God through the Word of that prayer. In fact, union with God through devotion is the whole purpose of reciting these prayers, or mantras.

In case you're not familiar with the term *mantra* as I use it, a mantra is a worded formula given to us by God through the sponsorship of an ascended master. It is a short, spoken prayer that can be easily memorized and repeated over and over. Each mantra invokes a particular aspect or quality of the Divinity, intensifying that action of God's Spirit in the one who gives the mantra. Because Saint Germain gave us this mantra, we have instant access to his Causal Body when we recite it with devotion.

As you give the mantra, imagine that you are hearing the voice of your Holy Christ Self saying these words within you. Close your eyes and accept the reality of your Christ Self. Feel the concentric rings of this mantra going out from you to the edges of the cosmos. Such is the power of mantra and of the spoken Word.

Unceasing Communion

The mystics taught that true prayer does not take place just at peak moments of the day or week. True prayer is unceasing communion with God even in the midst of daily activities. As Teresa of Avila said, we should talk with God about even the smallest concerns of our day. Our conversations with him can take place anywhere.

Sometimes we turn the dial of our minds to the concrete mind, the thinking mind, and let it sit there the whole day. It takes practice to turn the dial again in order to tune in to the devotional level, the level of God-consciousness, the level of Christ-consciousness, as easily as we change the frequency of a radio or TV.

It's important not to get locked into the consciousness of thinking man. There's more to us than thinking man and thinking woman. Saint John Cassian, a fifth-century monastic, wrote: "Through constant meditation on things divine and through spiritual contemplation,...the soul is caught up into an ecstasy." Through this practice, said Cassian, the soul can enter into such a close and continuous union with the Lord that "whatever we breathe or think or speak is God."[16] Try to put yourself in his place. He could write these words because he had such an experience.

This was also the path of Saint Thérèse of Lisieux. She once said, "I do not believe I have ever been more than three minutes at a time without thinking of Him."[17] Brother Lawrence, a seventeenth-century lay Carmelite, wrote:

> The time of business does not with me differ from the time of prayer; and in the noise and clatter of my kitchen, while several persons are at the same time calling for different things, I possess God in as great tranquillity as if I were upon my knees at the blessed sacrament.[18]

Brother Lawrence's example shows us that in the midst of the most physical work, in the act of balancing our karma, serving our fellowman, and fulfilling our life's calling, it is possible to be in that spiritually receptive mode of continual communion with God.

Teresa of Avila believed that the mystical encounter with God in our day-to-day business is no less valuable than the visions and ecstasies of the saints. "The Lord walks among the pots and pans," she said, "helping you both interiorly and exteriorly."[19]

In his First Epistle to the Thessalonians, Paul urged them to "pray without ceasing."[20] To me, unceasing prayer is like being in love. When you are in love, you are always thinking of the beloved. When you are in love with God, you can never take your attention off of him. You are consumed by a spiritual passion. Moments apart from him are an agony. Nothing else will comfort you but his love as he rekindles the fiery ecstasy of heart-to-heart communion. The psalmist cried out to the living God to express feeling so far from and outside of God in those moments when he is not in the very center of the fiery furnace of God's love:

> As the heart panteth after the water brooks, so panteth my soul after thee, O God. My soul thirsteth for God, for the living God: when shall I come and appear before God? My tears have been my meat day and night, while they continually say unto me, Where is thy God?...
>
> I will say unto God my rock, Why hast thou forgotten me?... As with a sword in my bones, mine enemies reproach me; while they say daily unto me, Where is thy God? Why art thou cast down, O my soul? and why art thou disquieted within me? hope thou in God: for I shall yet praise him, who is the health of my countenance, and my God.[21]

Prayers and Meditations

Establish a daily ritual of praying and communing with God. Seek his guidance and protection for yourself and for all who are in your care. You can pray alone or with your family. Morning is an ideal time and it doesn't have to take long. If you establish a connection with God first thing in the morning, you will find it much easier to stay connected to God during the day and your day will go better.

Developing the Practice of Interior Prayer

It takes a strong mind to hold steady a constant communion with God, whether in silent or audible prayer. One way to develop this practice is to pick a short devotional prayer and memorize it. Repeat it several times at first and build a momentum on it by giving it more often and with more repetitions. Continue to repeat it in your mind until its repetition is habitual and the prayer begins to repeat itself from the depths of your mind.

When you discipline your mind through this devotional practice you will discover, as the mystics did, that as you go about your daily activities your soul will travel through the mind and the heart over the inner Word that you recite. Allow that inner Word to carry you to the threefold flame within the secret chamber of your heart.

One easy mantra that can be used to establish communion with God is the refrain from the devotional prayer "Love Me":

> *As a rose unfolding fair*
> *Wafts her fragrance on the air,*
> *I pour forth to God devotion,*
> *One now with the Cosmic Ocean.*

Love Me

Visualize a pink rose unfolding in your heart as the Rose of Sharon, flooding you with the radiance of the Lord Jesus Christ and drawing to you from his Causal Body whatever is the need of the hour.

Beloved mighty I AM Presence and beloved Holy Christ Self, by and through the magnetic power of the immortal, victorious threefold flame and the adoration flame ablaze within my heart, I decree:

> 1. *I AM so willing to be filled*
> *With the love of God;*
> *I AM calling to be thrilled*
> *With the love of God;*
> *I AM longing so for grace*
> *From the heart of God;*
> *Yearning just to see his face*
> *By the love of God.*

> Refrain:
> *As a rose unfolding fair*
> *Wafts her fragrance on the air,*
> *I pour forth to God devotion,*
> *One now with the cosmic ocean.*

> 2. *I AM hoping so to be,*
> *Made by love Divine.*
> *I AM longing Christ to be,*
> *Wholly only thine.*
> *I AM so peaceful in thy love,*
> *Feel at home with God above.*

I AM at one with all mankind—
The cords of love God's children bind.
I AM fore'er one living soul
With angels, man, and God as goal.

3. *I AM locked in God's great love,*
   His mighty arms of power;
   Cradled now by heaven above,
   Protected every hour.
   I AM alight with happiness,
   Wholly filled with God success,
   For I AM love of righteousness.
   I love thee, love thee, love thee,
   My own God Presence bright;
   Love me, love me, love me,
   Protect me by thy might.
   Remain within and round me
   Till I become thy light!

PART TWO

The
Threefold Path:
Purgation
Illumination
Union

Purgation

CHAPTER 5

Forging Christhood

"Who is God? Who am I? And how can we unite through love?" The burning need the mystics felt to answer these questions and to achieve their ultimate end—union with God—led them to pursue a threefold path of purgation, illumination and union.

Saint Bonaventure, a thirteenth-century theologian and a disciple of Saint Francis, explained that in the purgative stage sin is expelled, in the illuminative stage the soul learns the imitation of Christ, and in the unitive stage the soul is day by day being united with God. Bonaventure said that in the purgative stage man comes to understand himself; in the illuminative, he comes to understand God; and in the unitive, he strives to be united with God. Some writers consider these stages to be a step-by-step path with each stage leading to the next. Others believe the stages can take place simultaneously and that not every mystic experiences every stage.

The word *purgation* refers to the process through which the soul is cleansed and made pure, purged of all that is unlike God. In this stage, the mystic seeks to purge his soul of all that separates him from God. Purgation comes to the soul only after she has experienced her awakening in God. This awakening brings joy to the soul. But when God's light and love suddenly enter the world of the mystic, he becomes acutely aware of his own faults and weaknesses. He sees his imperfections against the backdrop of God's perfection. More importantly, he sees that his imperfections, or sins, are what separate him from God and he can no longer tolerate the gulf.

At the Very Core of Mysticism Is Love

We'll begin our exploration of this notion with Saint John of the Cross, a sixteenth-century mystic and Doctor of the Church. To attain this title, a servant of God is required to show a high degree of sanctity and eminent learning and must be proclaimed Doctor by an ecumenical council or the Pope. Saint John was a profound contemplative, master theologian and poet as well as a busy reformer and administrator. In spite of extensive and severe trials, his life was one of complete dedication and deep inner peace and happiness.

Out of his intense experience Saint John gathered material for reflection and the ultimate construction of his mystical teaching. He lived as an example of all that he taught as the mystical way: "perfect union with God through love."[1] Although his writings are extensive, his mystical doctrine can be expounded in a few words:

> A man makes room for God by wiping away all the smudges and smears of creatures, by uniting his will perfectly to God's; for to love is to labor to divest and deprive oneself for God of all that is not God. When this is done the soul will be illumined by and transformed in God. And God will so communicate His supernatural being to [the soul] that it will appear to be God Himself

and will possess all that God Himself has....

The road leading to God does not entail a multiplicity of con-siderations, methods, manners, and experiences—though in their own way these may be a requirement for beginners—but demands only the one thing necessary: true self-denial, exterior and interior, through surrender of self.[2]

With these words Saint John is confirming that God is within the self, that God is the Self, and that pure love is that which is willing to be stripped of all that is less than God. How many of us can contemplate that goal and can appreciate what it takes and the sacrifices each day?

At the very core of mysticism is love; indeed, there can be, there is no mysticism without love. And love, as long as it is in the Mat-ter plane, includes in itself suffering. This is one of the very careful facts of the existence of love: If we are not willing to suffer, then we are not willing to love. The piercing of the soul and the piercing of the heart through suffering is part of the mystery of love.

When we take on the love of God and the love within our hearts, it becomes a burning, transmutative fire. It becomes a vor-tex so intense that it whirls as the fire infolding itself that Ezekiel ob-served.[3] Now this vortex of energy, whirling in its center, the more intense it becomes, the more it magnetizes, like a whirlwind, almost like a tornado, everything around itself into the flame. When we then call forth an intense light of any virtue of God, that light will also draw to itself energies that are diametrically opposed to it.

Why is this so? It is because the core of all creation is God, is fire, is sacred fire, and that white-fire core can never be tampered with. That which is misqualified is the energy in the spheres around the core, but the core, or nucleus, is an energy field of Spirit in matter. That energy is God and remains God but it is imprisoned in the matrices of imperfection in which we have encased it.

True love means that we love the light of God that is in the core enough to be willing to tangle with and transmute the misqualified energies that surround it. This is the meaning of God being crucified in matter. God's energy is encased in a mold of limitation formed by our prejudices, prides, jealousies, greed, selfishness, and so forth. We have the ability to superimpose that mold, or energy veil, upon the nucleus because we have free will and thus are co-creators in the planes of Matter.

So the soul that truly loves God chooses to set free this misqualified energy. And that is what we are doing when we give violet-flame decrees, prayers and invocations. When we invoke the sacred fire, we have two factors of magnetization. First, we magnetize a tremendous energy of sacred fire from God; and second, at the same time, we are expected to hold and focus that energy to "consume" the darkness we have created by transmuting those energies into light.

There are many souls who find the teachings of the ascended masters or the path of sainthood, and their first contact, after many years of searching, is one of great joy and happiness. As if coming upon a crystal waterfall in the mountains, they dance and play in the cool, clear waters. But once they begin to build the momentum of sacred fire, they realize that it carries a tremendous responsibility.

For the fifteenth-century saint Catherine of Genoa, the awakening to God came after years of loneliness and depression in an unhappy marriage. Her biographer recounts that Catherine had reluctantly gone to make her confession at the urging of her sister when "suddenly, as she knelt before [the priest] she received in her heart the wound of the unmeasured Love of God." Imagine this transfer of love being of such high vibration and intensity that it felt like a piercing, as though she had been wounded. Catherine had so clear a vision of her own misery and her faults, and of the goodness of God, that she almost fell upon the ground. And by these sensations of infinite love, and of the offences that had been done against this most sweet God, she was so greatly drawn by purifying affection away from the poor things of this world that she was almost beside herself, and for this she cried inwardly with ardent love, "No more world! No more sin!"...

She returned home, kindled and deeply wounded with so great a love of God...she seemed beside herself.... Her hatred of herself was more than she could endure.[4]

From the time of this experience and for the next four years, Catherine walked the road of purgation.

Conquering the Lesser Self

Catherine of Genoa and other mystics have described the process by which the soul overcomes her impediments and reunites with God as a purgatory of having to stay at a certain level in order to be purged of the very substance of that level. "As the soul makes its way to its first state [the pristine state of her creation]," she said, "its ardor in transforming itself into God is its purgatory."[5]

These words are not an exaggeration. To truly face and conquer the lesser self is arduous. We should not underestimate the challenge. We should know what we are getting into when we want to go all the way back to God in this life. This is what the apostle Paul meant when he said, "I die daily."[6] Paul saw a part of himself dying daily, and some of those parts he was attached to. Some of those parts he didn't necessarily want to see die. But as Christ was formed in him, something else that was not the Christ had to die.

Catherine of Genoa explained that what dies daily is not the soul but portions of the lesser self. She wrote:

I see rays of lightning darting from that divine love to the creature, so intense and fiery as to annihilate not the body alone but, were it possible, the soul.

These rays purify and then annihilate [that which was impure].... The soul becomes like gold that becomes purer as it is fired, all dross being cast out.... What is obliterated and cast out is not the soul, one with God, but the lesser self.... Once stripped of all its imperfections, the soul rests in God.[7]

Author Serge Hughes remarks that Catherine of Genoa "unquestionably belongs to the great and almost universal tradition of spiritual writers who...see [the spiritual life] as a way or a process. She is engaged in a journey, a continued struggle for perfection, or, to use her favorite analogy, an endless battle between the false self and the true self."[8]

"Every day," said Catherine, "I feel that motes are being removed, which this Pure Love casts out...all the time God does not cease to remove them."[9]

Catherine saw the darts of love descending from her mighty I AM Presence, entering and purging her. She felt motes being removed by God's love. All this she experienced. The purgative process is like the seven days of Creation, resting the seventh day. It's our re-creation in the image and likeness of Christ. Because we have created unwisely, incorrectly, ignorantly, so we have to first uncreate before we can re-create. When the process is complete, our soul rests in God.

When we surrender to God and give ourselves to him for this process, his position is: "Get it over with as quickly as possible. I want you home to my heart. I want to give you all of myself. I am your divine Lover. I am your Husband, your Bridegroom. Come home to me." God knows that we suffer in the process. So if we give all of ourselves to him, he steps up the process so that we can get through the pain to the bliss.

Testing, Trials and Temptations

During the process of purgation, the soul faces testing, trials and temptations that come in many guises. It is in the crucible of testing that the virtues of Christhood are forged. There is no other way to forge your Christhood than in the crucible of testing.

Some mystics experienced the fires of purgation through the censure of their religious superiors. Meister Eckhart, Mechtild of Magdeburg, Jacob Boehme, John of the Cross, Teresa of Avila and Symeon the New Theologian were all at some time in their life suspected of questionable beliefs or called on the carpet for their teachings. Some were persecuted and imprisoned. This was because they were so close to God that they were becoming one with him and they dared to affirm that.

Whatever were the outer reasons and motives behind the privations, misunderstandings, imprisonment and persecutions of the mystics, their suffering served as part of the set in the drama they played, part of the stage that the Great Dramatist arranged to wean them from outer attachments.

In our soul's ascent to perfection, we will all pass through the labyrinth of our karma, facing our human creation that at times appears almost to obliterate the light of the Christ and the light of the Presence. We walk as in the dark, groping. We cannot see. We grope our way only by faith, trusting that if we keep on keeping on we shall arrive.

Prayers and Meditations

Dynamic Decrees Access God's Light

The prayers in this section are meant to be given aloud. They are dynamic decrees, the most powerful method of accessing God's light. When we decree, we are not only communing and asking God for help—we are, in effect, commanding the flow of energy from Spirit to matter. With all prayer forms, devotion is a key to accessing the spiritual power that can change our world and the world around us.

Decrees can be considered spiritual letters. Most decrees are composed of a greeting, or preamble; a body; and a closing. We begin by naming our I AM Presence and Holy Christ Self in order to tap into our full God-potential. Saints, masters and angels named in the preamble help bring about what we are requesting when our requests are in accordance with God's will. When you begin a session of decrees, you can give the following preamble or formulate your own:

> *In the name of my I AM Presence and Holy Christ Self, I call to the hosts of heaven to direct God's light, energy and consciousness to bless all of life. I ask my I AM Presence to adjust my requests in accordance with what is best for my soul and the souls of those for whom I am praying.*

The body of the decree contains our command for a specific action of light to manifest in the world. It is the request for help from our Christ Self and the great heavenly beings. The body of the decree can be repeated as many times as desired to increase its effect by focusing more light on our request.

The closing of the decree seals the action of precipitation, causing light to descend tangibly into matter according to God's will. Many decrees use a formal closing such as this one:

> *And in full Faith I consciously accept this manifest, manifest, manifest! (3x) right here and now with full Power, eternally sustained, all-powerfully active, ever expanding and world enfolding until all are wholly ascended in the light and free! Beloved I AM! Beloved I AM! Beloved I AM!*

Violet Fire and Tube of Light Decree

You are now ready to invoke dynamically the "Violet Fire and Tube of Light Decree." The tube of light builds a foundation of spiritual energy. Because it establishes a powerful connection with God, this decree is often given at the beginning of a session of prayer and decrees.

This decree is complete in itself, including its own preamble and closing. In honor of the Indwelling Presence of God and to more fully visualize the light being invoked, it is customary to stand while giving it.

Visualize yourself standing inside a tube of light, nine feet in diameter, as it descends from the heart of your God Presence. (See page 35 for a depiction of the soul standing inside the tube of light.) Give the decree with profound love for God and with confidence that he hears your prayer and answers.

> O my constant, loving I AM Presence, thou light of God above me whose radiance forms a circle of fire before me to light my way:
> I AM faithfully calling to thee to place a great pillar of light from my own mighty I AM God Presence all around

me right now today! Keep it intact through every passing moment, manifesting as a shimmering shower of God's beautiful light through which nothing human can ever pass. Into this beautiful electric circle of divinely charged energy direct a swift upsurge of the violet fire of freedom's forgiving, transmuting flame!

Cause the ever expanding energy of this flame projected downward into the forcefield of my human energies to completely change every negative condition into the positive polarity of my own Great God Self! Let the magic of its mercy so purify my world with light that all whom I contact shall always be blessed with the fragrance of violets from God's own heart in memory of the blessed dawning day when all discord—cause, effect, record, and memory—is forever changed into the victory of light and the peace of the ascended Jesus Christ.

I AM now constantly accepting the full power and manifestation of this fiat of light and calling it into instantaneous action by my own God-given free will and the power to accelerate without limit this sacred release of assistance from God's own heart until all men are ascended and God-free in the light that never, never, never fails!

I AM Presence, Thou Art Master

This dynamic decree is especially useful for protection. Ask your God Presence for protection for yourself, your family and others. Repetition builds momentum, thus making your decrees more effective, so try giving this decree nine times each morning. As you give it, you may feel yourself becoming one with your I AM Presence.

See the light of your God Presence descending into your form and transforming it into the image of God. Imagine the blue light-ning, which represents protection, flashing forth from your I AM Presence. This blue lightning is an intense form of spiritual energy that dissolves negative energy on contact.

> *I AM Presence, thou art Master,*
> *I AM Presence, clear the way!*
> *Let thy light and all thy power*
> *Take possession here this hour!*
> *Charge with victory's mastery,*
> *Blaze blue lightning, blaze thy substance!*
> *Into this thy form descend,*
> *That perfection and its glory*
> *Shall blaze forth and earth transcend!*

I thank you and I accept it done this hour in full power according to God's will. Amen.

CHAPTER 6

The Dark Night of the Senses

ome mystics have described a certain element of the purgative process as a "dark night." Saint John of the Cross said that there are two dark nights: the dark night of the senses and the dark night of the Spirit. The dark night of the senses takes place during the purgative stage and as a transition into the illuminative stage. The dark night of the Spirit takes place before the ultimate union of the soul in Christ in the spiritual marriage. I will address the dark night of the Spirit later, in the context of the spiritual betrothal.

Author E. W. Trueman Dicken writes: "Night is simply the saint's term for 'privation,' eradication of attachment to all that is not God, and it is by this progressively more complete privation that the soul is finally emptied of all that can fill her to the exclusion of God."[1]

Saint John called this journey toward union with God a night because at its beginning "the individual must deprive himself of his appetite for worldly possessions. This denial and [self-]privation is like a night for all his senses."[2]

Saint John of the Cross

The individual no longer derives joy or fulfillment through the senses although he remembers how it was when the things of the world did bring him joy. In this night, the soul is pushed within to experience God without the perceptions of the senses.

"The means or the road along which a person travels to this union," Saint John said, "is faith, and for the intellect faith is also like a dark night."[3] The intellect is always demanding reasons and asking questions, always curious, always taking the knife of the intellect and carving up into minutia the details of this world. But the walk to God is by faith. It has no explanation except the soul within longing to be one with the Great Lover.

The final reason for calling the journey toward union with God a night is that "the point of arrival, namely, God," said Saint John, "is also a dark night to man in this life."[4]

At times during our return journey to God we reach very high states of God consciousness and we may come out of them momentarily not knowing who we are or where we are. When this happens, it is because there are no coordinates in time and space to which we can relate our union with God. We experience the presence of heavenly beings, feel their radiation, and may be caught up for hours at a time in this rapture only to come out from it again. And so, to be in this rapture one moment and in the next moment to be back in the world is like a dark night because there is no point of relativity.

One of the first experiences I had of the infinity of God and of the self swallowed up in it is this: I was caught up into a realm where I suddenly saw myself and experienced that I was, as it were, breaking through the level of the clouds as one does when flying in an airplane. And then all was stillness, the stillness of an immensity. The clouds went on for an infinity and no one else was there, no one else at all. It was an entire cosmos, simply an immensity. In order to enter this vastness, I had to go alone. And so, entering into it was almost like a night because it was the total stilling of all existence as I had known it previously. There was no one and no thing to relate to but simply the immensity.

In moments like this, the thought comes to the soul, "Shall I withdraw?" There is a moment of decision: "Shall I turn back? Or shall I go on? Shall I pursue this course uncharted?" For that is what it is—uncharted. Though we can read what the saints have written, when we ourselves have the experience we have the sense that there is no one there.

Increasing Attachment to God

Dicken writes, "It is by this progressively more complete privation that the soul is finally emptied of all that can fill it to the exclusion of God."[5] Most people do not know the experience of being totally filled with God, and therefore to give up the known for the unknown is not easy. To be totally filled with God does not mean that you need to live a cloistered existence. It is far greater a challenge to be in the world yet not of it, to be filled with God and to be one of those radiating points of light like runners extending from the heart of Christ.

When you are filled with God as divine love, God will give you everything that you lawfully need and that you lawfully want. I urge you to consider that your life will be far greater in joy when there is no room in you for anything but God. Because God is everything. God is everything that is real. Everything you could ever want, he will bring to you. As Mary Baker Eddy, the founder of Christian Science, said, "Divine Love always has met and always will meet every human need."[6]

During the dark night of the senses, the mystic disciplines himself to overcome inordinate desires—desires that do not lead to his union with God. How can you tell what is an inordinate desire? It is a desire that enslaves you, that you return to, that you cannot be free of, a desire in which you are not the master of both yourself and the desire. As Saint John of the Cross advised, "To come to possess all, desire the possession of nothing."[7] That is, if you want to possess all of God, *if you really want that*, desire the possession of nothing and God will give you his All.

This does not mean that we cannot love one another. It means that rather than being a possessive love, our love for one another becomes an intense love for God in one another. The mystics recognized as one of the primary laws of spiritual progress that as the soul becomes increasingly detached from the things of this world, she becomes increasingly attached to God.

I have found that God uses a very interesting way in which to wean us from the world: He lets persecutions come upon us abundantly. This was true in the lives of many of the mystics. When we experience the persecutions and we see what the world is capable of, somehow we lose a certain zest for the world and we desire instead the most profound oneness with God.

To bring us Home faster, I think God gives us a little bit of his spur by allowing us to experience some good kicks here and there. He lets our persecutions also be the means of bearing and balancing karma. In the midst of adversity we get a tremendous sense of co-measurement between the self that is God here and the Self that is infinite and beyond all the pettiness of the planet.

The Imitation of Christ

Saint John of the Cross outlined ways to help the disciple get through the dark night of the senses. He said that by two steps alone the soul could conquer all desires that separate her from God. First, the mystic should have a "habitual desire to imitate Christ in everything that he does." He should meditate on Christ's life "so that he may know how to...behave in all things as Christ would behave."[8]

Jesus himself gave us the assignment to be an imitator of his work: "Verily, verily, I say unto you, He that believeth on me, the works that I do shall he do also; and greater works than these shall he do; because I go unto my Father."[9] If Jesus is giving us this assignment, then he must know that God has placed within us the resources to fulfill it.

And to this end we can ask, "What would Jesus do?" Actually, what Jesus would do isn't automatic or obvious. Jesus never turned aside from challenging evil, either embodied evil or impersonal evil. He never walked away from it and he never indulged it. Thus, to know what Jesus would do, read the Gospels over and over again, because you will find that Jesus had different responses for different types of people. Also read the Gnostic gospels and, if you like, listen to my lectures on Gnosticism, because the Gnostic gospels show a different face of Jesus than you see in the four Gospels.

The Holy Christ Self, detail,
Chart of Your Divine Self

Another important resource is *The Imitation of Christ* by Thomas à Kempis, a fifteenth-century mystic. This book is one of the best known Christian books on devotion, and it explains how to gather the virtues of Christ and demonstrate them in your life.

In summary, to master the basic principles of life that Jesus taught, learn everything you can about what he did in his life. Contemplate how and why he did it, and then make your decision about what you would do in a similar situation. This is how we learn the imitation of Christ, which Saint John of the Cross says is the first step for getting through the dark night of the senses.

John's second step is this: "Every pleasure that presents itself to the senses, if it be not purely for the honour and glory of God, must be renounced and completely rejected for the love of Jesus Christ, Who in this life had no other pleasure, neither desired any, than to do the will of His Father."[10]

John is not trying to engender shame or guilt or fear or control. He is simply stating facts of the law of the path to becoming one with God. He explains that "appetites sap the strength needed for perseverance in the practice of virtue. Because the force of the desire is divided, it becomes weaker than if it were completely fixed on one object."[11] One goal that I have set for myself is to have nothing that I do, hour by hour throughout my life, that I cannot dedicate to the honor and glory of God. I am certain that you are also striving to achieve this goal.

The path of the imitation of Christ is the path of the Christian mystics. Jesus said: "If any man will come after me, let him deny himself, and take up his cross daily, and follow me."[12] To deny ourselves means to deny the lesser self, the carnal mind. To take up our cross daily means to take up the cross of our karma. I counsel individuals to not let the sun go down, not let their head come to rest on their pillow until they have dealt with the karma that has descended that day, meeting that karma with violet flame and service, with love and every positive response.

Taking up our cross daily also means taking up the cross of our divine plan, which is our duty to be who we really are as we walk in the footsteps of Jesus on the path of personal Christhood. Jesus said, "Whosoever will save his life shall lose it: but whosoever will lose his life for my sake, the same shall save it."[13]

Those who symbolically lose their life for Jesus in this embodiment find it again in this embodiment. They find it by the greater light that enters their temple and by the Holy Christ Self that descends upon them. Losing your life doesn't necessarily mean dying, although those who die in the Lord certainly find their life again in the Lord, either on earth or in heaven. But in this life we give up many things to follow in Jesus' footsteps, and in the course of doing so we find our true life.

Paul said, "Bear ye one another's burdens, and so fulfil the law of Christ."[14] When we lose ourselves in service to others, we find that as we nourish the fires of Divinity in them, our life as God individualized in Spirit is also increased. Think what a glorious feeling it is to conclude a day and know that by communion with another soul we have been able to turn that soul around and direct her back to God.

Finding Resolution Within

Saint Philip Neri wrote, "Nothing more glorious can befall a Christian than to suffer for Christ."[15] We might ask, How can suffering be glorious? When we understand that suffering for Christ means bearing our karma ourselves so that he doesn't have to bear it for us, we begin to see suffering from a different perspective.

When we refuse to carry our karma and to balance it, we are in effect demanding that Jesus carry it for us. The truth of the matter is that the crucifixion of one Son of God two thousand years ago does not deliver any of us from accountability for our disobedience to the laws of God. Jesus Christ lived that we might learn the lesson of balancing the conditions of our sin through the sacred fire of the Holy Spirit and through personal accountability. Thus we are saved, not in the sense of the absolution of our karma, but in the sense that we have been taken on by Jesus, we have been supported by Jesus. He goes through the atonement for our karma even as we must work out that karma, every jot and tittle of the Law.

The apostle Paul affirmed the law of karma when he said, "Let every man prove his own work, and then shall he have rejoicing in himself alone, and not in another. For every man shall bear his own burden."[16] Thus, if we are angry or unkind, the responsibility for that act does not fall upon the crucified Saviour. As it fell from our own tree of free will, so we will reap the consequences. The Christ in us can deliver us when we forsake that condition and when we invoke the sacred fire of the Holy Spirit to bless the part of life we have wronged.

Therefore, my answer to the question "How can suffering be glorious?" is that balancing our karma, paying back our debts to God and to every part of life that is God, one by one, is glorious! Because none of us is truly happy deep down inside and neither can our souls be truly happy until we have undone the wrongs we have done to any part of life that is God—all the way back to the beginning of time and our first incarnation. We must balance our debts.

Outstanding karmic debts can burden and depress us. They are one cause of psychological problems. The original meaning of the word *psychology* is "the study of the soul." Coming to grips with our psychology and seeking resolution in our relationship with our inner child is part of the process of our soul's attaining union with God. So let's not insulate ourselves from our pains, our discomforts, our psychological problems, our burdens. Let's not attempt to avoid dealing with them or think that we can simply push them away if we will just give enough violet flame.

The violet flame is a miracle solvent, and many painful records can be consumed by the flame. But on the path of self-mastery we also need to master our psychology, and sometimes we need help to resolve certain issues. So let's allow them to come up to the surface where we can look at them, dissect them, pray about them and implore God to heal them. Let's go deeper than our outer form. We can go to our heart and our soul without fear that we'll lose our identity if we open ourselves and allow the Holy Spirit to come in and show us the problem. God loves each one of us intensely, and the moment we really want to make it, the whole universe will rush in to help us.

Making Things Right Leads to Union

We each need to also watch our own mind and heart and desire body. And that is because sometimes, although we may not know it, at a certain level of our being we simply refuse to bear the responsibility for our karma. An example of this is the vast number of lawsuits today where people attempt to collect money from others because they fell down in their yard or some such thing. We never heard of such lawsuits until the twentieth century, and they are on the rise.

The reason people want someone else to pick up the tab for their misfortunes is because the law of karma is not taught in the West. This is also why some of the nations of the West have gone into socialism. The thinking is that the government should pay the bill for everything that happens to the individual. Well, having someone else pick up the tab only postpones the day when the individual will have to deal with his personal karma.

If we as individuals and as nations refuse to bear responsibility for our words and deeds, if we are not willing to suffer the consequences of our words and deeds, this, then, becomes the boulder of pride and rebellion against the laws of God that prevents our soul's reunion with God. It is possible to get into a national, local or personal consciousness where we do not see what befalls us or what we do as our personal responsibility.

The saints and adepts who willingly underwent what we perceive to be extreme torments, self-imposed afflictions or severe illnesses were balancing their personal karma (perhaps in the only way they knew how) in order to achieve their soul's realignment with God. Sometimes, through intense physical and emotional suffering, they were balancing planetary karma as well. Those who walk the path of the mystic do eventually go beyond merely bearing their own karma to also bearing "Christ's karma."

What is Christ's karma? It's the karma of the whole world, and Jesus has been carrying it for us for two thousand years. How about saying to Jesus, "Let me bear world karma, Lord." Isn't it about time he had some lightbearers and Christed ones on the earth who will help him carry world karma? We can do it.

We are called to this path because God loves us and knows that we need this path and this teaching, we need the violet flame and we need to live a life of service so that we can meet all the people to whom we owe a debt where that debt must be paid back personally. Many debts can be paid back with the violet flame, but others simply cannot be paid without personal interaction.

Each time we make things right with someone who has suffered needlessly because of our senseless doings, we achieve union, great or small, with the God in that person. As long as we are enmeshed in a spiral of negative karma with the outer self (our outer self and someone else's) we cannot know true oneness with the Inner Self of them or us. Each time we balance the karma for it, we have eliminated some substance that was between us and someone else. We have united with the God in them and opened a channel whereby they can unite with the God in us. That's what balancing karma means.

When we are engaged in paying debts to life, it may at times feel as if all of life is drudgery and that we should instead be doing something great and creative and original and wonderful. But the truth is that we create that drudgery for ourselves by making karma. And when we do, we need to get down on our knees and scrub and scrub and scrub.

What It Means to Give Yourself to God

The alleviation of the suffering of one soul and many souls is my reason for being. It doesn't matter to me who has caused the suffering; I desire to relieve all life of the burdens of unnecessary suffering. Suffering is sometimes necessitated by the law of karma. But wherever God's laws allow it, I want to be there to help relieve others' burdens, to transmute their pain through understanding and compassion, to lead them out of the darkness of limited self-knowledge in the lesser self into the light of unlimited Self-knowledge in the Greater Self. This, for me, is what makes life worth living. If I can't do this every day, I wonder why I am walking the planet.

If this brings me closer to God and I balance personal and planetary karma in the process, well and good. But that's not what's important to me. For me, suffering through the balancing of personal and planetary karma is not a suffering at all. It is pure joy. And if there be pain, it is transmuted into the bliss of my union with God in every part of life.

The reason to bear suffering is the very joy of bearing another person's burden, not for what it gets us, not because it gets us to union with God—leave that to God. The reason to bear suffering is the very joy of the moment of giving the God flame to another, not because of some benefit we will receive.

I think that I am goal-oriented. Whatever it takes to achieve the goal, I can suffer, or endure, because I see the end from the beginning. When I was in college, I used to put a sign on my books that read "This too shall pass." And I would visualize the day and date when I would be through. I told myself, "There's really no distance between where I am now and where I'll be then. It will pass." That little mantra eliminated time and space for me, and before I knew it I had graduated from college.

I'm glad I embraced the school of hard knocks—the school of purging, illumining and uniting with my heart under the tutelage of my spiritual mentors. It is a school of the most profound love. I tell you truly, anyone who goes to the trouble of disciplining you and expending all the fire of his heart and being and soul to make you the person that he knows you really are, as my mentors did for me, is a true friend and teacher. Go after such ones, because they're your real friends.

Jesus said that he laid down his life for his sheep, the lost sheep (souls) of the house of Israel. When you determine to help people you do lay down your life, your light—all that you are, heart and essence. That's because it takes that much love and that much proving to God that you really want to be the instrument for the saving of souls, whether a single soul or many.

I welcome you to the opportunity to save the souls on this planet who will never be touched or reached unless they are touched by you. You are a unique person. Wherever you are in the world, you will come in contact with people that may never again in this life contact someone who has a tie to the ascended masters, who has the key to opening the door so that they can make it. Always be aware of that.

Once when I had an opportunity to counsel a certain group of people, I recognized that if I hadn't taken the time to speak with them, there would have been nowhere else for them to go to come to an understanding of who and what they were then—and of what they had to do in order to get to be who they really are.

It is a great feeling to know that God has called you to a particular service, to know that if you are listening in your heart you will hear God saying to you: "If you don't speak to this person, no one else will. How else will I contact them? How else will I bring them home? They have nowhere else to go, no one else to teach them, no one else to save them."

When you realize that this is what it means to give yourself to God—to know such tremendous joy of helping people and facilitating their entering the courts of heaven—I assure you, there is nothing in this world that you cannot easily give up in exchange for such immense gladness. That's the only way I can describe it, immense gladness that you have really been useful to the universe.

Transmuting Karma through Service and Prayer

The writings of the mystics tell us that there comes a moment on the purgative path when the intense suffering abates. The flame of love swallows up some aspect of the lesser self and the soul moves on to a new level.

For example, at that crucial point in her life when Catherine of Genoa was consumed by dismay at her imperfections, she began to suffer from a constant sense of sin. For four years she fasted and put herself through mortifications—which are more or less severe penances and disciplines. Suddenly one day the thought of these mortifications was in an instant taken from her mind and she was unable to continue them.

A similar moment came in the life of the fourteenth-century Dominican friar and mystic Henry Suso. Suso's biography entitled *The Exemplar* explains that he put himself through harsh ascetic practices for sixteen years and then stopped abruptly and completely when "an angel appeared to him on Pentecost Sunday with the welcome whisper that God wanted him to discontinue this manner of life."[17] Thereupon, Suso shifted his emphasis from mortification to detachment.

This fashion of the earlier saints to mortify themselves was an act of penance and suffering that symbolized following in the footsteps of Jesus in the hour of his crucifixion. This was their way of bearing the sins of the world in the imitation of Christ. In the lives of the early mystics, suffering ceased when the soul had learned certain lessons and a certain block of karma had been balanced.

Although suffering is a part of the purgative process and a known place on the path of initiation, you don't have to flagellate yourself. If you're suffering in and through something, which means enduring it—just use the violet flame and serve God. The ascended masters don't recommend or condone the practice of physical mortification. Rather, they teach that when we strive to serve life and to share with others their teachings on the path to reunion with God, when we give our all to the liberation of the souls of the planet and offer a daily ritual of decrees and prayer, it is enough. They teach that we must take care of our health and lead a balanced, wholesome life. What is important is not to be a martyr but to be a strong, fiery spirit in a strong, fiery body.

When your negative karma is descending and accelerating because God is pushing you to get through it faster, transmute it by invoking the violet flame. When there's work to be done for the LORD, that's the time and the way to give your all in sacrificial service. This can be a marvelous, exhilarating, self-transcending experience. And afterwards, give your body the full rest it needs. All of us together are working in our own way and in our own karmic situation to bring about the moment in the planet when the leaven of the Divine Mother leavens the consciousness of the entire world.

Prayers and Meditations

The Keeper's Daily Prayer

"The Keeper's Daily Prayer" is a meditation upon your true identity as a flame of God. It is the prayer of those who keep the flame, the divine spark, on behalf of all life. Helios and Vesta represent the Godhead to all souls evolving on the planets orbiting the sun. Their God consciousness sustains our physical solar system. The Great Central Sun is the center of the cosmos, the point of origin of all physical and spiritual creation.

As you recite the words, visualize the merging of your consciousness with the divine spark within your heart and within the heart of God. See yourself becoming the flame, one with the essence of all life.

A flame is active—
A flame is vital—
A flame is eternal.

I AM a God flame of radiant love
From the very heart of God
In the Great Central Sun,
Descending from the Master of Life!
I AM charged now
With beloved Helios and Vesta's
Supreme God consciousness
And solar awareness.

Pilgrim upon earth,
I AM walking daily the way
Of the ascended masters' victory

That leads to my eternal freedom
By the power of the sacred fire
This day and always,
Continually made manifest
In my thoughts, feelings,
  and immediate awareness,
Transcending and transmuting
All the elements of earth
Within my four lower bodies
And freeing me by the power
  of the sacred fire
From those misqualified foci of energy
 within my being.

I AM set free right now from all that binds
By and through the currents
  of the divine flame
Of the sacred fire itself,
Whose ascending action makes me
God in manifestation,
God in action,
God by direction and
God in consciousness!

I AM an active flame!
I AM a vital flame!
I AM an eternal flame!
I AM an expanding fire spark
From the Great Central Sun
Drawing to me now every ray
Of divine energy which I need
And which can never be requalified
  by the human

And flooding me with the light
And God-illumination of a thousand suns
To take dominion and rule supreme forever
Everywhere I AM!

Where I AM, there God is also.
Unseparated forever I remain,
Increasing my light
By the smile of his radiance,
The fullness of his love,
The omniscience of his wisdom,
And the power of his life eternal,
Which automatically raises me
On ascension's wings of victory
That shall return me to the heart of God
From whence in truth
I AM come to do God's will
And manifest abundant life to all!

I AM My Brother's Keeper

In our journey on the mystical path, we come to realize that we are our brother's keeper. Jesus said, "I am in my Father, and ye in me, and I in you."[18] Because Christ is in every son of God, it follows that as we draw forth the radiance of God, we also give of that radiance to all of his creation. This prayer is an affirmation of our brotherhood with all of God's children:

I AM my brother's keeper.
O God, help me to be
All service and assistance,
Compassion just like thee!

I AM my brother's keeper.
O Jesus, by thy flame
Of resurrection's blessing
Give comfort in thy name!

I AM my brother's keeper,
O Presence of God so near,
The fullness of thy blessing,
Pure divinity appears!

I AM my brother's keeper,
The guardian of his flame;
In quiet power and knowing,
I love him in thy name!

Prayers for Protection

Archangel Michael is the most revered angel in Jewish, Christian and Islamic scripture. He and numberless angels under his command protect the children of God from every kind of physical and spiritual danger.

Throughout the day, whenever you feel the need to reinforce God's protection around yourself or around those who may be suffering, you can stop and summon immediate assistance from Archangel Michael by giving a fiat. A fiat is a short, powerful exclamatory statement that calls forth God's light. Give this fiat with fervor and love to instantaneously invoke the protection of Archangel Michael:

Archangel Michael, Help me! Help me! Help me!

Traveling Protection

While we can invoke angelic intercession with a short fiat, it's best to give decrees to Archangel Michael daily, ideally in the morning, for the protection of yourself and loved ones throughout the day. You can also give them at night for protection while your soul travels out of your body during sleep.

"Traveling Protection" is easy to memorize, and you can give it anytime you feel the need for protection from harm or negativity. Also give it whenever you travel. Visualize Archangel Michael and his legions surrounding every vehicle and its occupants as well as every pedestrian. Give the decree three or more times:

> *Lord Michael before, Lord Michael behind,*
> *Lord Michael to the right, Lord Michael to the left,*
> *Lord Michael above, Lord Michael below,*
> *Lord Michael, Lord Michael wherever I go!*
>
> *I AM his love protecting here!*
> *I AM his love protecting here!*
> *I AM his love protecting here!*

CHAPTER 7

An Accelerated Path to Soul Freedom

The mystics who experienced severe trials, illnesses and persecutions were balancing karma, both personal and planetary, in the best way they could for the times in which they lived. Even amidst their greatest sufferings, the mystics saw their path as one of pure joy, for they experienced that they were drawing ever closer to God. Thérèse of Lisieux, whose short life included intense suffering, is said to have remarked, "I have reached the point of not being able to suffer any more, because all suffering is sweet to me."[1]

The law of karma may bring some suffering to our doorstep. But today there is a path that can minimize suffering and that is the path of the violet flame—Saint Germain's gift to mystics in the Aquarian age. With the violet flame, instead of our having to encounter all of the old karmic situations and take a million years to work through that karma physically, we have the opportunity to accelerate our homeward journey.

Sometimes the most suffering we have to bear is to give our dynamic decrees long enough to get the action of transmutation rolling at a peak alchemical pitch. At times this might take fifteen minutes, at other times an hour or longer. When we do reach that peak, we may even feel ourselves pushing through to a new plane of awareness.

The violet flame, given by us with full intensity, fervor and ardor on behalf of the entire planet, is a way of balancing much karma. By applying God's laws and giving dynamic decrees to the violet flame, we can to a large extent free ourselves of the burdens of our personal karma. In addition, by applying ourselves in prayer for and service to others, we can help to free them and the world.

A Powerful Tool That Frees Energy, Restores Harmony

What makes the violet flame such a powerful tool? In our physical world, violet light has the highest frequency in the visible spectrum. As Fritjof Capra explains in *The Tao of Physics*, "violet light has a high frequency and a short wavelength and consists therefore of photons of high energy and high momentum."[2] At spiritual levels, that high-frequency energy of the violet flame can consume the debris within and between the atoms of our being. It's like soaking them in a chemical solution that, layer by layer, dissolves the dirt that has been trapped there for years.

Freed of this dross, the electrons begin to move more freely, thus raising our spiritual vibration and our energy levels. This action takes place at nonphysical dimensions of matter. As energy is repolarized and transmuted, it becomes part of our storehouse of positive energy.

There is not one of us that doesn't regret and wish we could undo some moment of our life, some action, some unkind word. By working with the violet flame, we can send the flame of the Holy Spirit to deliver both the one we have wronged and ourselves of the burden. As the violet flame passes through the emotional, mental and physical layers of our being, it transmutes the cause, effect, record and memory of anything less than perfection and restores that energy back to its natural state of harmony with Spirit.

Saint Germain tells us that the violet flame is the most physical of all flames. When we invoke it, transmutation occurs at all levels. The flame can expel toxins lodged in physical organs and can transmute the records of present and past lives.

Physical healing may come about through the use of meditation and the Science of the Spoken Word and also through proper diet, which is most important. It is the light in our body temple that brings about a manifestation of healing. Since so many physical conditions are caused by mental and emotional problems, the healing of the mind and emotions and the erasing by the violet flame of records in the subconscious is often all that is required to eliminate physical suffering.

We go to causes behind effects. That doesn't mean to say we don't call upon the medical profession and use medicines and whatever is necessary, including surgery, for the correction of conditions in the body. But ultimately we seek to manifest the victory wherein the mind of God within us controls the manifestation in matter.

In essence, the violet flame affords us a path of minimum suffering. When we invoke it through our prayers, it can help ease the process of resolving karma and trauma. It can even enable us to balance some of our karmic debts without directly encountering those involved. The violet flame is a sacred fire that renews us, helping to make us more whole.

Invoking the Violet Flame

How do you invoke the violet flame? At the most simple level, you can give a mantra where you affirm the name of God, I AM, and then declare that that I AM is the violet flame right where you are. One mantra that I like to give to increase the manifestation of the violet flame in my aura is this: *"I AM a being of violet fire! I AM the purity God desires!"* It is meant to be repeated over and over as a mantra that sings in your heart. The more you give it, the stronger the action of transmutation you are building.

You can recite this mantra and any of the mantras and decrees in this book once, three times or as many times as you want until you feel your heart responding to the healing power of love that comes through the violet flame. You can also create your own variations of this mantra wherever you perceive the need for a higher resolution in any situation, as shown in the two examples that follow the basic mantra.

> *I AM a being of violet fire!*
> *I AM the purity God desires!*
>
> *My heart is alive with violet fire!*
> *My heart is the purity God desires!*
>
> *My family is enfolded in violet fire!*
> *My family is the purity God desires!*

This little mantra becomes a meditation and a visualization that is anchored in the physical temple by the spoken Word. Giving word to our thoughts and our feelings through the throat chakra is the means whereby we gain a new dimension from our prayers, because it is through the throat chakra that we bring into the physical form that which is in the mind and the heart. This is why, when people begin to give these mantras, they experience an immediate acceleration of consciousness. The violet flame, then, is the first step on the path of the soul's return to the Spirit, or to the I AM Presence.

Our God Is a Consuming Fire

We see references to God as a sacred fire throughout the Old and New Testaments. As recorded in the Book of Deuteronomy, Moses said to the children of Israel: "The LORD thy God is a consuming fire."[3] John the Baptist, heralding the coming of Jesus Christ, prophesied: "One mightier than I cometh, the latchet of whose shoes I am not worthy to unloose. He shall baptize you with the Holy Ghost and with fire."[4] It is this baptism of the sacred fire that we seek, and we always begin seeking it within.

When we meditate upon the sacred fire in the heart, we soon discover that a pulsating light comes clearly to our consciousness. This light accelerates to a vibration, or frequency, that reads as the color violet, hence the term *violet flame*. This flame, an aspect of the Holy Spirit, has been seen by seers, mystics and saints, and in the Aquarian age the time has come for its realization and application.

I AM the Violet Flame

With this mantra, given to us by Saint Germain, we can call forth the violet flame from his heart to saturate ourselves and our loved ones, all of life and the entire planet. As with all decrees, you can give this once, three times, or as many times as you like.

> *I AM the violet flame*
> *In action in me now*
> *I AM the violet flame*
> *To light alone I bow*
> *I AM the violet flame*
> *In mighty cosmic power*
> *I AM the light of God*
> *Shining every hour*

I AM the violet flame
Blazing like a sun
I AM God's sacred power
Freeing every one

The Gift of Freedom in the Age of Aquarius

Saint Germain sponsors our use of the violet flame. He petitioned the heavenly councils to give the lightbearers of the world access to the violet flame for the accelerated balancing of karma. The condition under which they granted the dispensation was that Saint Germain would pay the price if people misused it. Think of the sacrifice he made to make that commitment! He knew that some would misuse the flame, yet he was willing to take that burden upon himself for the sake of those who would use it for the blessing of all mankind and for their personal victory in the light.

How is it possible to misuse the violet flame? Using it to transmute past karma and then repeating those actions or acting in a manner that is not forgiving or loving to any part of life is a misuse of the flame. So is engaging in anything that violates the principles of freedom, mercy and forgiveness—the alchemical powers in the violet flame.

Thanks to Saint Germain's intercession, through the alchemy of the violet flame the unredeemed, unperfected soul can become a partaker of the divine nature here and now in this life. By our invocation of the violet flame, by our meditation upon the flame, and by bathing our consciousness in the flame, we can experience that transmutation, that change of energy and consciousness which was so often promised by the Hebrew prophets—the promise of forgiveness, the promise that "though your sins be as scarlet, they shall be as white as snow."[5]

The promise of the forgiveness of the Holy Spirit is our only way out of the state of nonalignment, our sense of sin. We get back into alignment by the power of God to erase sin. The Holy Spirit breaks down the misqualified energies or the misuses of life that we have brought forth by our misuse of free will. For example, hatred is a misuse of free will. We have free will to qualify God's energy as love or as hatred. If we have qualified it as hatred, that energy rests with us and remains with us as part of our consciousness until we transmute it by love.

The power of the Holy Spirit to transmute hatred into love manifests by this dispensation of the violet flame. Violet flame decrees transmute and soften the burdens of the day and begin to transmute the accumulation of the past. The violet flame can be used to transmute, or change, any negative energy in our lives. We can also use it to produce positive change in all areas of human life, whether personal or planetary.

> *Lovely God Presence, I AM in me,*
> *Hear me now I do decree:*
> *Bring to pass each blessing for which I call*
> *Upon the Holy Christ Self of each and all.*
>
> *Let violet fire of freedom roll*
> *Round the world to make all whole;*
> *Saturate the earth and its people, too,*
> *With increasing Christ-radiance shining through.*
>
> *I AM this action from God above,*
> *Sustained by the hand of heaven's love,*
> *Transmuting the causes of discord here,*
> *Removing the cores so that none do fear.*
>
> *I AM, I AM, I AM*
> *The full power of freedom's love*
> *Raising all earth to heaven above.*

Violet fire now blazing bright,
In living beauty is God's own light

Which right now and forever
Sets the world, myself, and all life
Eternally free in ascended master perfection.
Almighty I AM! Almighty I AM! Almighty I AM!

Transmuting Karma Alchemically

Sometimes people make mistakes. Sometimes they make vows to God and then unwittingly and unthinkingly break them. Please know that if this happens to you, it does not make you a miserable sinner. You have an altar in your heart and you may have a physical altar as well. So if you have erred, go quickly to your altar as soon as you recognize your error. Call on the law of forgiveness. Decree for fifteen minutes or a half hour and be done with it.

When you condemn yourself, you place yourself outside of the circle of God. As long as you remain in a state of self–condemnation, you keep yourself outside of the circle of God. So if you have things that you condemn yourself for, go to the altar, confess them all. If you do it again, go to the altar, confess them again. If you find yourself repeating this loop again and again, consider getting help from a therapist to look at your psychology, your background, your childhood, your relationship to your parents. Invoke the violet flame and engage in service to balance your karma. Call on the law of forgiveness every time you condemn yourself. And then you'll be able to jump right back into the circle of God. God forgives you even before you ask him for forgiveness.

The Law of Forgiveness

Beloved mighty victorious Presence of God, I AM in me,
beloved Holy Christ Self and beloved Heavenly Father:
In the name and by the power of the Presence of God
which I AM and by the magnetic power of the sacred fire
vested in me, I call upon the law of forgiveness and the vio-
let transmuting flame for each transgression of thy Law, each
departure from thy sacred covenants. Restore in me the
Christ Mind, forgive my wrongs and unjust ways, make me
obedient to thy code, let me walk humbly with thee all my
days.

In the name of the Father, the Mother, the Son and the
Holy Spirit, I decree for all whom I have ever wronged and
for all who have ever wronged me:

> *Violet fire enfold us! (3x)*
> *Violet fire, hold us! (3x)*
> *Violet fire, set us free! (3x)*

> *I AM, I AM, I AM surrounded by*
>   *a pillar of violet flame,*
> *I AM, I AM, I AM abounding in*
>   *pure love for God's great name,*
> *I AM, I AM, I AM complete*
>   *by thy pattern of perfection so fair,*
> *I AM, I AM, I AM God's radiant flame*
>   *of love gently falling through the air.*

> *Fall on us! Fall on us! Fall on us!*
> *Blaze through us! Blaze through us!*
>   *Blaze through us!*
> *Saturate us! Saturate us! Saturate us!*

> *I accept this done right now with full power! I AM this*
> *done right now with full power! I AM, I AM, I AM God-life*
> *expressing perfection all ways at all times. This which I call*
> *forth for myself I call forth for every man, woman, and child*
> *on this planet!*

There is an alchemy in these spoken decrees whereby, as in no other form of prayer, misuses of God's energy are transmuted. This means that each time we give mantras that contain the name of God, the substance of God's energy that we once qualified with negativity, or darkness, is being requalified with light.

The Inner Meaning of Communion

The lower figure in the Chart of your Divine Self (opposite page 34) shows us that we can become the temple of God as we invoke the violet flame from our mighty I AM Presence (the upper figure) through our Holy Christ Self (the middle figure). It is a profound teaching of the mystical path of Christianity that we must go through the Son to get to the Father.

We don't necessarily think of Jesus as having used the violet flame, but consider the first miracle he wrought: At the marriage feast in Cana of Galilee, Jesus turned water into wine. Esoterically, this symbolizes the turning of the water of the human consciousness into the wine of the Spirit. Wine is a purple or violet color, and this is a clue that Jesus was using that aspect of the Holy Spirit that is the frequency of the violet flame. Teresa of Avila wrote that Jesus gave her a ring set with a stone that resembled an amethyst as a token of their spiritual marriage. I believe he put within that stone the frequency of the violet flame in order to carry her forward on her path.

The violet flame is also symbolized in the wine used in the

ritual of Holy Communion. The inner meaning of the word *communion* is "come ye into union." Through this ritual, as we are washed in the wine of forgiveness, a portion of our Divine Reality is restored, bringing us closer to union with Christ and the I AM Presence.

Radiant Spiral Violet Flame

When you invoke the sacred fire, you don't have to be aware of your own sins, or your own past, or your past incarnations. You don't have to know how this all came about. All you need to know is that when you invoke the fires of the Holy Spirit in the name of God and Christ, those sacred fires will descend. This is a more certain law than any we are aware of in our science, in our mathematics, in our day-to-day life.

In the name of the beloved mighty victorious Presence of God, I AM in me, and my very own beloved Holy Christ Self, I decree:

> *Radiant spiral violet flame,*
> *Descend, now blaze through me!*
> *Radiant spiral violet flame,*
> *Set free, set free, set free!*
>
> *Radiant violet flame, O come,*
> *Expand and blaze thy light through me!*
> *Radiant violet flame, O come,*
> *Reveal God's power for all to see!*
> *Radiant violet flame, O come,*
> *Awake the earth and set it free!*
>
> *Radiance of the violet flame,*
> *Expand and blaze through me!*

Radiance of the violet flame,
Expand for all to see!
Radiance of the violet flame,
Establish mercy's outpost here!
Radiance of the violet flame,
Come, transmute now all fear!

Prayer for World Peace

Through prayer and meditation, you can also direct the violet flame into conditions in your community or on the world scene—such as pollution, political turmoil or war—to transmute their karmic causes and bring resolution and peace. You can dedicate any of the prayers and decrees in this book as well as the following prayer to bring about the highest resolution in any situation you name.

O violet flame, O violet flame, O violet flame!
In the name of God, in the name of God,
in the name of God!
O violet flame, O violet flame, O violet flame!
Flood the world, and flood the world
and flood the world!
In the I AM name, in the I AM name,
in the I AM name!

Peace and peace and peace
be spread throughout the earth!
May the Orient express peace,
May the Occident express peace,
May peace come from the East and go to the West,
Come from the North and go to the South,
And circle the world around!
May the swaddling garments of the earth

Be in place to magnify the LORD
In this day and hour and this night.
May the world abide in an aura of God peace!

*And in full faith I consciously accept this manifest, man-
ifest, manifest! (3x) right here and now with full power, eternally sustained, all-powerfully active, ever expanding, and
world enfolding until all are wholly ascended in the light and
free! Beloved I AM! Beloved I AM! Beloved I AM!*

Sealing the Energies of Prayer

The closing of a decree or a session of decrees seals the action
of precipitation that causes light from Spirit to descend tangibly
into matter. As in the closing that follows the "Prayer for World
Peace," the closing of a decree signifies your acceptance of what
you have called forth. Give it with just as much intent and intensity as you have given the decrees. Doing so seals the tremendous
energies you have invoked through them. Here is another closing
you can use:

*I accept this done right now with full power. I AM this
done right now with full power. I AM, I AM, I AM God life
expressing perfection all ways at all times. This which I call
forth for myself I call forth for every man, woman and child
on this planet.*

Fitting Prayer and Decrees into Your Life

Since a package of our karma arrives on our doorstep each
morning, many people like to give their violet-flame decrees
before their day begins. As with all forms of prayer, you will derive

the greatest benefit from the violet flame and other decrees if you set aside a specific time each day to decree without interruption. At times you may find it necessary to decree for an hour or longer to reach that peak alchemical pitch where you can feel that you're transmuting negative energy into light.

But you can give your decrees anywhere, anytime—in the shower, in your sacred space, while doing chores or before going to bed. Simply repeating a violet-flame mantra anytime you feel tense, tired or irritated can make a difference. If you have a job or other responsibilities that take you from morning till night and you never seem to stop, use the shorter decrees that are in this book. Commit them to memory and then, when you're in a rush, give them powerfully once, seal yourself in that power, and do not let it go for the whole day. You can demonstrate God without changing your entire lifestyle. It just takes some juggling.

A powerful way to decree is with a group. When you gather with others to offer decrees, the power of your decrees is squared by the number of individuals present. This is a tremendous dispensation given to us by the ascended masters. Through another dispensation, this power is then multiplied by the power of the ten thousand-times-ten thousand. So the more people who are decreeing together in one place, the more you are acting in a concerted effort where everyone receives a greater descent of light. That's one benefit of having a group in your hometown with whom you can decree.

The power of multiplication is understood through these words of Jesus: "Again I say unto you, That if two of you shall agree on earth as touching any thing that they shall ask, it shall be done for them of my Father which is in heaven. For where two or three are gathered together in my name, there am I in the midst of them."[6]

CHAPTER 8

Fasting on the Spiritual Path

In addition to the violet flame, fasting is another effective way in which we can accelerate the process of purgation. Saints and mystics through the ages have fasted as a very natural inclination and response to God—the desire to be self-emptied for a more profound and sensitive communion with God. It is absolutely true that when you set aside the denser foods, you open the way for a much greater inner peace and a greater communion with the lights of all eternity.

Saint John Climacus wrote of the virtues of fasting: "Detachment from the things perceived by the senses means the vision of things spiritual.... Fasting ends lust, roots out bad thoughts, frees one from evil dreams. Fasting makes for purity of prayer, an enlightened soul, a watchful mind, a deliverance from blindness. Fasting is the door of compunction,...joyful contrition and end to chatter, an occasion for silence, a custodian of obedience,... health of the body, an agent of dispassion, a remission of sins, the gate, indeed, the delight of Paradise."[1]

Fasting is advocated in the spiritual traditions of East and West. It has been a regular practice among Christian monastic communities. For instance, the Poor Clares of San Damiano ate only one full meal a day except on Sundays and Christmas, when they were allowed to have two full meals. (The Poor Clares were an order founded in the thirteenth century by Saint Clare, a disciple of Saint Francis.) In addition, the Pope forbade the Poor Clares to eat any meat. Clare, however, showed discretion in her fasting rules. She explained that exceptions should be given for "younger sisters, those who are weak, and those who are serving outside the monastery.... In a time of evident necessity," she said, "the sisters are not bound to corporal fasting."[2]

Purging Toxins, Building Health

Many people who have entered the spiritual path have felt the need to fast and to change their diet, eliminating fatty meats and dairy products. The denser foods inhibit the ability of the individual cells of the body to carry light.

Of course, you have to know when and what to fast on under the supervision of your health practitioner as well as your spiritual teacher. Keep in mind that the goal of fasting and a good diet is to purge toxins so that you can build health. It takes a strong and vibrant body to work the works of God on earth. The eleventh-century Eastern Orthodox priest Ilias the Presbyter understood the need for balance. He wrote:

> The ascetic has to know when and by means of what foods to treat the body as an enemy, when to encourage it as a friend, and when to succour it as an invalid. Otherwise he may unwittingly offer to the friend what is proper for the enemy, or to the enemy what is proper for the friend, and to the invalid what is proper for either of

the other two; and having alienated all three he may find them fighting against him in time of temptation.[3]

Lightening Consciousness, Healing Form

The reason I urge students on the Path to learn about and pursue a dietary program that includes both cleansing and rebuilding the body is that we need every hour of every day of our assigned allotment of years. That allotment was given to us by God when we took embodiment. We were told what our life span would be and that we could increase it by good works and a spiritual life, or we could decrease it by eating the wrong diet, indulging in wrong vibrations, taking in alcohol, drugs and nicotine, and so forth. Wonderful souls have shortened their lives and consequently forgone their ascension, their ultimate union with God, because they didn't have enough time in this world to fulfill the requirements in that life. Others have extended their lives by ten or fifteen years.

Somewhere along the spiritual path many people decrease their intake or stop eating heavy fats and foods that can burden the heart and other organs. But just because a person has stopped eating the wrong foods does not mean that the various organs of the body are being purged of the accumulated substances from those foods. A good cleansing program that is appropriate for the current condition of your body is an important adjunct to a change in diet. Your health practitioner can help you choose one that will be right for you.

It can be difficult to be on a cleansing program or to maintain a healthy diet when you have to do all the cooking yourself. But when you cook your own food you are putting your own vibration into it, and you can also cook what is right for your body. Your diet can be elaborate or simple, but the ideal purpose of it is to build and maintain health and longevity. There will be times when you make exceptions and that's fine. While you won't benefit if your exceptions become the rule, you also don't need to be fanatical or rigid.

Many who bring their diet into alignment experience a lightening of their consciousness and a healing of their form. Should you choose to undertake a change in your diet, consider having a photograph taken of yourself before you begin so that you can track your progress. Take another photo a year later and compare the two to see what changes have resulted. Be sure to celebrate your victory!

The Alchemy of Blessing Food

The transformation of matter by the alchemy of the Holy Spirit through the ritual of Holy Communion is altogether present and real. We can apply the same alchemy that is involved in the blessing of the Communion wine and bread to the blessing of our food and drink and those who grew and prepared it. When we bless our food, the Presence of God within us charges that food with a flame that goes all the way to the fiery core of the atoms within it, charging the matter and molecules with the energy of the Holy Spirit.

This is the ritual I use for the blessing of food and drink:

Place your left hand under the food and your right hand over it. If you are blessing a large quantity of food, either place your hands above the food or stand with the palms of your hands facing the food. You can do the very same thing with a glass or any quantity of whatever liquid you partake of.

While your hands are so engaged, ask your mighty I AM Presence and Holy Christ Self to demagnetize the food and drink of impurities, toxins and pollutions and to charge them with the light of God and specifically with the energy currents of healing and the properties needed throughout the body of those who will be partaking of that food.

As you continue to practice this ritual each time you eat or drink, you will find that you receive much more than just the nutritional and other properties of the food. When you begin by calling for the demagnetization of impurities from the food, you are asking for the emptying of the molecular chalice, which is what food is, so that it can then be filled with the light and energy you need.

Fasting from the Senses

The Bible and the writings of the mystics show that in addition to fasting for health, fasting as spiritual discipline and atonement are well-established spiritual practices. Fasting is a means of regulating the body and mind so that they are not distracted or disturbed. If we would speak to God in his holy mountain, we must come apart and be a separate people.

In many ways, our society is addicted to noise. Sometimes people fill all the empty spaces in their day with the TV set, the radio or just plain chatter. Besides attending spiritual retreats, there are simple practices we can incorporate into our daily lives whereby we can achieve a stilling of the mind. For example, we might decide to turn off the TV set for a month, or we might take a rest from continually absorbing information through reading or other forms of news and entertainment. By withdrawing our attention from the communications and entertainment of the world, we create an opening to discover and commune with the part of us that is eternal.

Idle chatter is one of the most deadly enemies to our spirituality. Useless words expend precious energy. Not only do we drain our energy through excessive speech, but sometimes we make karma by saying things we later wish we had not said or by gossiping or speaking negatively, disparagingly or with criticism, and so forth. So don't be afraid to have moments of silence in your life. Don't be afraid to be alone or to have periods when no one is talking to you and you're not talking to someone else. Be alone with God and find out how strengthening that is.

Many saints and mystics have undergone voice fasts where they did not speak for days or longer at a time. Members of certain monastic communities live under a perpetual vow of silence. They understand that speaking consumes energy. In fact, the spoken word is so powerful that when we misuse it we feel depleted. We all know how we feel when we've talked and talked and talked all day—we don't want to talk anymore because we're absolutely spent. By having days when we speak cordially to people but don't get engaged in long conversations one after the other all day long, week after week, we conserve the sacred fire within our energy centers.

It's also important to take time to be silent, as many of the mystics have done. The ascended masters encourage their students to do periodic voice fasts where they set aside a day or longer to be silent. You can use the practice of voice fasting to strengthen, heal and elevate yourself.

On your day of silence, pin a little note to your shirt that reads "Voice Fast." You'll find that in many circumstances you can even do a voice fast at work. Carry an erasable board and a marker and write down any necessary communications. Simply don't talk for a day. Give yourself this discipline and you'll see how much more energy you have that you used to spend on talking. Keep a listening ear so that at all times you are attentive to the still, small voice within—the voice of your Mentor, your Holy Christ Self.

Prayers and Meditations

Meditation on Self

This prayer for fasting is an affirmation of what you are when you are empty of all but God.

> *I AM no blight of fantasy—*
> *Clear-seeing vision of the Holy Spirit, Being!*
> *Exalt my will, desireless Desire,*
> *Fanning flame, inspired fire, glow!*
> *I will be the wonder of thyself,*
> *To know as only budding rose presumes to be.*
> *I see new hope in bright tomorrow here today—*
> *No sorrow lingers, I AM free!*
> *O glorious Destiny, thy Star appears,*
> *The soul casts out all fears*
> *And yearns to drink the nectar of new hope:*
> *All firmness wakes within the soul—*
> *I AM becoming one with thee.*

Sweet Surrender to Our Holy Vow

God cannot do any more for us than the level of our own surrender to him. In this prayer, we surrender to him and to our Holy Christ Self as the Divine Lover of our souls, who receives us only to take us to his heart and perfect us that we might attain our goal of complete union with him. Surrender is sweet. We surrender joyously to God and to full participation in God's being. And by our surrender we become that which we have always been.

Meditation upon the God Flame:

Our will to thee we sweetly surrender now,
Our will to God flame we ever bow,
Our will passing into thine
We sweetly vow.

Affirmation of the God Flame
merging with the heart flame:

No pain in eternal surrender,
Thy will, O God, be done.
From our hearts the veil now sunder,
Make our wills now one.

Beauty in thy purpose,
Joy within thy name,
Life's surrendered purpose
Breathes thy holy flame.

Grace within thee flowing
Into mortal knowing,
On our souls bestowing
Is immortal sowing.

Thy will be done, O God,
Within us every one.
Thy will be done, O God—
It is a living sun.

Bestow thy mantle on us,
Thy garment living flame.

Reveal creative essence,
Come thou once again.
Thy will is ever holy,
Thy will is ever fair.
This is my very purpose,
This is my living prayer:

Come, come, come, O will of God,
With dominion souls endow.
Come, come, come, O will of God,
Restore abundant living now.

Count-to-Nine Decree

This decree has a rhythm like a march. Just as the rhythm of an army marching in step can collapse a bridge, so the rhythm of a decree can create a strong spiritual force that breaks down accumulations of negative energy, habit patterns and undesirable karma.

Use this decree to control strong emotions, to get yourself in alignment, to strengthen your obedience to the directives of your Holy Christ Self. Use it to develop the practice of thoughtful deliberation, of considering the ramifications of your actions to others and the rippling effect they have throughout the planet. "Count-to-Nine" brings God-control of the mind to think logically, unemotionally, perceptively. Use this decree if you feel out of sorts, if you're having trouble making a decision, or if you don't know which road to take. Before you give it, appeal to your Holy Christ Self for guidance.

Although you can give this decree any number of times, the exercise outlined here calls for giving it nine times in all. To begin, you give it three times slowly and intensely. With this very intense type of decreeing you are setting a strong forcefield, using the words to build a house, so to speak, in which you are secure and in control of your energies. The image of a house is a good visualization to use with this decree.

Once the house is built, you ignite a flame in the fireplace by picking up the speed for the next round of three repetitions as you visualize a blazing violet-flame fire in the fireplace.

Now the violet-flame fire is roaring. As you say the final round of three repetitions, visualize yourself casting into the flame everything that's not of God. See the violet fire consuming it all, then see the flame expand and lovingly enfold you and fill the whole house. See violet-flame angels caressing you, bathing you, bringing you into alignment and giving you such eternal peace that you can go back to anyone, anywhere, anyplace and be the ultimate peacemaker because you have the peace of God in your heart through the violet flame.

In the name of the beloved mighty victorious Presence of God, I AM in me, and my very own beloved Holy Christ Self, I decree for peace and harmony throughout my entire being and world:

> *Come now by love divine,*
> *Guard thou this soul of mine,*
> *Make now my world all thine,*
> *God's light around me shine.*
>
> *I count one,*
> *It is done.*
> *O feeling world, be still!*
> *Two and three,*
> *I AM free,*
> *Peace, it is God's will.*

I count four,
I do adore
My Presence all divine.
Five and six,
O God, affix
My gaze on thee sublime!

I count seven,
Come, O heaven,
My energies take hold!
Eight and nine,
Completely thine,
My mental world enfold!

The white-fire light now encircles me,
All riptides are rejected!
With God's own might around me bright
I AM by love protected!

I accept this done right now with full power! I AM
this done right now with full power! I AM, I AM, I AM
God-life expressing perfection all ways at all times. This
which I call forth for myself I call forth for every man,
woman, and child on this planet!

Illumination

CHAPTER 9

Visions and Revelations

In the illuminative stage, the mystic's life is focused entirely on God. His sole desire is to be with God and to serve God. This stage, one of profound concentration and contemplation, is often marked by visions, ecstasies, revelations, raptures and other phenomena. Father John Arintero tells us: "Those who believe that the life of mystics is gloomy and sad, filled with sensible obscurities and strewn with crosses, do not know what true happiness is.... Indescribable consolations and the wonderful illuminations...are interwoven amid the many trials."[1]

As mysteries are unlocked, the mystic gains a new perspective on his relationship with God and with his fellow men. He experiences a greater sense of the Presence of God. His soul mounts to new heights of joy in communion with her Lord.

Symeon the New Theologian, an eleventh-century Byzantine poet and saint of the Eastern Orthodox Church, experienced raptures and visions. Of one vision, Saint Symeon wrote: "What word can describe this!... I see a light which the world does not possess. Sitting in the cell I see within me the Creator of the world and talk with him and love him and am nourished only by the Knowledge of God."[2]

As I interpret this, he saw the Creator seated on the throne in the secret chamber of the heart. He saw the threefold flame, and saw it as God. And the Creator also talked with him and loved him, and he was nourished by the Knowledge of God.

Illumined with Complete Understanding

The twelfth-century mystic Hildegard of Bingen described how she was infused with the light of illumination:

> In the year 1141...a flaming light of great brightness from the open heaven completely flooded my brain, heart, and breast like a flame that does not burn but warms.... Immediately I was illuminated with a complete understanding and exposition of books like the Psalter and other Catholic tomes, both of the Old and New Testament.... I did not perceive these visions in dreams or sleeping, or in a trance, nor with exterior ears of man or in hidden places, but by God's will, beheld them wide awake and clearly, with the mind, eyes, and ears of the inner man.[3]

Like Hildegard, other mystics have revealed that the soul experiences God through spiritual senses that are beyond the physical senses and the intellect. Through their spiritual senses, mystics have heard or seen God the Father, Jesus, the Blessed Mother or angels. Joan of Arc was guided by the voice of Saint Michael the Archangel. Francis of Assisi, kneeling before an image of the crucified Christ in the Church of San Damiano, heard the Lord urging him: "Francis, go and repair my house" (the universal Church). Catherine of Siena conversed with God the Father in a state of ecstasy and while in this state she dictated her spiritual

Saint Francis of Assisi, detail from a fresco by Cimabue.

treatise, *The Dialogue*. This *Dialogue* was a dictation from God to Catherine, faithfully recorded by her secretaries.

Recognizing His Presence

Other mystics did not see visions but unmistakably felt the Presence of God. Teresa of Avila's later life was guided by these inner visions and by *locutions*, the term she used to describe directions, revelations and rebukes from God. Teresa said she never saw any of her visions with her bodily eyes but rather with "the eyes of the soul"[4] and she only twice heard God's messages with her bodily ears. She explained that sometimes "the Lord puts what He wants the soul to know very deeply within it, and there He makes this known without image or explicit words."[5]

Origen of Alexandria observed: "We do not think that God speaks to us from outside. For those holy thoughts that arise in our heart, they are the way God speaks to us."[6] The twentieth-century mystic Mother Teresa of Calcutta said she left her position as a high-school teacher to work in the slums because she heard the call of God while on her way to an annual retreat in Darjeeling, India. "The message was quite clear," she said. "I was to leave the convent and help the poor whilst living among them. It was an order."[7]

Saint Bernard of Clairvaux, a twelfth-century mystic, said he recognized that Christ had entered his soul only by the movement of his heart. He wrote:

> I confess...that the Word has visited me, and even very often. But although He has frequently entered into my soul, I have never at any time been sensible of the precise moment of His coming.... He is living and full of energy, and as soon as He has entered into me He has quickened my sleeping soul, has aroused and softened and goaded my heart, which was in a state of torpor and hard as a stone....
>
> It was...only by the movement of my heart that I was enabled to recognize His presence, and to know the might of His power by the sudden departure of vices and the strong restraint put upon all carnal affections.[8]

Teresa of Avila's description of her first vision is also very instructive:

> Being in prayer on the feastday of the glorious St. Peter, I saw or, to put it better, I felt Christ beside me; I saw nothing with my bodily eyes or with my soul, but it seemed to me that Christ was at my side—I saw that it was He...who was speaking to me.[9]

Teresa said visions like these are "represented through knowledge given to the soul that is clearer than sunlight. I don't mean that you see the sun or brightness, but that a light, without your seeing light, illumines the intellect so that the soul may enjoy such a great good."[10]

She added that this vision of Christ helped her to avoid

Saint Teresa of Avila

displeasing God because she felt Jesus was always looking at her. The mystical experience, Teresa of Avila teaches, is open to all. "If the soul does not fail God," she said, "He will never fail...to make His presence clearly known to it."[11] She also said that the mystic is keenly aware that his experiences are gifts from God. He cannot produce them although he can prepare himself to receive them.

Visualizing Christ Within

One of Teresa of Avila's techniques for communing with Jesus was to imagine the figure of Christ within her. This is a perfect imaging. Who she was visualizing was not only her Lord Jesus but the Indwelling Christ, her Holy Christ Self. In her autobiography, she wrote:

> It used to happen, when I represented [visualized] Christ within me in order to place myself in His presence, or even while reading, that a feeling of the presence of God would come upon me unexpectedly so that I could in no way doubt He was within me or I totally immersed in Him. This did not occur after the manner of a vision.[12]

As an adjunct to Teresa of Avila's exercise of visualizing Christ within, you can meditate on the aura of Jesus or the saint or ascended master of your choosing. With focused attention, visualize that brilliant light around you. Doing this can help you to draw forth the intensity of your own Christ-radiance that is stored in your Causal Body. Because heaven respects your free will, the saints and masters will not enter without your invitation. So, along with this visualization, call to Jesus to enter your being to cleanse you with the fires of his Sacred Heart.

Jesus, I bid you enter my whole temple now!
By my free will, by my God-dominion, I welcome you!
And I let go of everything, my Lord.

Also know that whichever heavenly being you commune with or visualize, the result will always be that your Holy Christ Self will also enter your temple and draw nigh to you.

Phenomena and the Mystical Path

Teresa of Avila was candid when writing about her visions, locutions and raptures. She said that during her raptures, without her being able to resist, her soul was carried off. Sometimes even her body levitated. Levitation, Teresa said, happened to her rarely but when it did it distressed her because she feared it would increase her notoriety. One time Teresa was attending a service along with some ladies of nobility and she began to levitate. She wrote:

> I stretched out on the floor and the nuns came and held me down; nonetheless, this was seen. I begged the Lord very much not to give me any more favors that would involve any outward show.... He was pleased to hear me because up to the present I have never had this experience again.[13]

In her *Dialogue*, Catherine of Siena recorded this instruction
God gave her about levitation:

> The body is lifted up from the ground because of the perfect union
> of the soul with me [God], as if the heavy body had become light.
> [This does not happen] because its heaviness has been taken away
> but because the union of the soul with me is more perfect than the
> union between the soul and the body. And for this reason the
> strength of the spirit united with me lifts the body's weight off the
> ground.[14]

It is popular today to equate mysticism with raptures, ecstasies,
visions or even levitation. But the Christian mystics often warned
that phenomena are not the goal of the mystical path. They said it
is dangerous to ask God for such experiences or to expect or wish
for them, because doing so leaves us open to projections from our
own imagination or from the devil.

Author J. Mary Luti writes:

> Although [Teresa] esteemed mystical phenomena, she was also
> cautious about them. She was cautious not only because such ex-
> periences could be counterfeited…, but also and especially be-
> cause she understood the mystical life to involve much more than
> peak experiences…. For Teresa, the marks of true Christian inti-
> macy with God were first, last, and always the marks of concrete
> love: the bearing of the cross [that is, personal and planetary
> karma], the service of neighbor. Sensation was not what she was
> seeking but transformation in God for the sake of God's service.[15]

Instead of being concerned with phenomena, the miracles that
we should be concerned with are the ones that manifest in our lives
and day-to-day happenings—the miracles of greater and greater
awareness of God. The goal is to attain a greater realization of
God. It is also possible, and it has happened in the lives of saints

The Angels' Kitchen, *by Bartolomé Murillo*

and seers of both East and West, that extraordinary manifestations can occur, such as levitation, visions, revelations and the stigmata. Many mystics have demonstrated spiritual gifts, such as the gift of healing. But the world's great mystics have always warned against becoming preoccupied with phenomena, because the goal of the spiritual path is not phenomena but oneness with God.

Prayers and Meditations

Becoming Light

The aura is a luminous emanation, or electromagnetic field, that surrounds the physical body. It registers the impressions, thoughts, feelings, words and actions of the individual and also regulates and reflects the health, vitality and longevity of the physical body. Science has shown that all sentient life emits an aura.

In sacred art, the aura is depicted as a halo of radiant light surrounding the head or body of Christ and the saints and angels. As an individual develops Christ consciousness, his aura begins to resemble that of the saints. The aura marks the circumference of a man's awareness of God, and its size is directly related to his God-mastery. The greater the size of an individual's aura, the more God can release his consciousness through it into the planes of Matter. This is because the aura is the coordinate in time and space of the Great Causal Body of God.

Exercise for Increasing the Light of the Aura

This visualization for sealing the aura can be used by itself or at the beginning of any session of decrees, prayers or meditation. When you give the "I AM Light" decree, feel the deep desiring of your soul to be liberated. This is why we decree—to liberate our soul. Give it humbly and with devotion, yet also with fervor, determination and a deep desire to close entirely the gap between your soul and God. When you decree in this manner, you set a mighty forcefield of protection around yourself that comes from your I AM Presence and turns aside discord and negative energy.

Sit in a quiet space where you will not be disturbed. Close your eyes. Visualize your threefold flame expanding within the secret chamber of your heart. Feel the great love of your soul for the Indwelling Presence of God living within you. From the very depths of your being, pour forth your devotion, love, gratitude and worship. Allow the joy and gratitude you feel to immediately take you to a higher level and vibration.

Now seal yourself and your consciousness in a globe of white fire. See your entire body sealed as though it were inside of a giant, radiant sphere of white fire, cloudy yet very firm. This mighty sphere of light is sealing you for your meditation. When you are set in the heart of devotion, affirm from deep within the threefold flame and from deep within your soul, with utter humility and devotion:

"I AM Light"

I AM light, glowing light,
Radiating light, intensified light.
God consumes my darkness,
Transmuting it into light.

This day I AM a focus of the Central Sun.
Flowing through me is a crystal river,
A living fountain of light
That can never be qualified
By human thought and feeling.
I AM an outpost of the Divine.
Such darkness as has used me is swallowed up
By the mighty river of light which I AM.

I AM, I AM, I AM light;
I live, I live, I live in light.
I AM light's fullest dimension;
I AM light's purest intention.

I AM light, light, light
Flooding the world everywhere I move,
Blessing, strengthening, and conveying
The purpose of the kingdom of heaven.

As you visualize the white-fire radiance around yourself, don't focus on your supposed imperfections or on any errors in your thought or consciousness. Don't allow yourself to concentrate upon any negative quality or condition. Instead, as you repeat this exercise regularly, see what the light can do for you. See how even your physical appearance can change, how a strengthening of the bonds of your health can occur in body, mind and spirit.

O Flame of Light Bright and Gold

Use this mantra to invoke the fullness of divine illumination from the spiritual sun into your being and world and to flood all with the golden flame of Christ illumination, understanding, perception and peace from the heart of God's own omniscience.

O Flame of Light bright and gold,
O flame most wondrous to behold,
I AM in every brain cell shining,
I AM in Light's wisdom all divining.
Ceaseless, flowing fount
    of Illumination flaming,
I AM, I AM, I AM Illumination.

CHAPTER 10

Experiences of the Mystics

he experiences of the mystics tell us something about the path to union with God. An experience that for me represents the illuminative stage came in the life of Henry Suso after the angel of God told him to stop his self-imposed torments because he needed to make progress in a different manner. This is what his biographer records:

> It happened once that he was seated in his cell...reflecting on spiritual matters. As he pondered the wonders of Eternal Wisdom, his senses were stilled in ecstasy and it seemed to him that a princely young man drew near and spoke to him: "You have spent enough time in elementary school. You are ready to take up higher studies. Follow me; I will conduct you to the spiritual graduate school [the highest school that exists in the world[1]], where you will be instructed.... This will establish your soul in holy peace and bring your devout beginning to a blessed end."
>
> [Henry] jumped happily to his feet and it seemed to

him that the young man took him by the hand and led him...into a spiritual land.... After walking across a meadow they entered a schoolhouse and were received with open arms by the students. When the headmaster heard the uproar being made over this would-be disciple, he said in true professional style, "Before accepting him as a pupil, I must question him personally."

After a short interview the headmaster announced to the student body: "This undergraduate has within him the seed of a first-rate scholar. But whether the seed will sprout or lie fallow depends on himself; if he is willing to be pulverized by the constant friction of hard work and stringent rules, luscious fruit will result from the seed of his dead self."

[Henry], not understanding the meaning of these words, turned to the young man who had acted as his guide and questioned him: "Dear companion, tell me more about this graduate school and the higher studies one pursues there."

"The science learned in the advanced school of holiness," said the young man, "is nothing else than a complete, perfect resignation of oneself, so that a man's will is so evenly balanced that the scale turns neither to the right nor left when God places on it joy or suffering, directly or through creatures. Man must strive earnestly to remain as steadfast in this total renunciation of self as is possible to human weakness, and to look only at God's honor and glory, imitating in this Christ's continual hunger for his heavenly Father's glory."

This explanation satisfied [Henry]. Hence, he resolved to put it in practice, cost what may, and to submit to all the school's regulations.... After a few minutes [Henry] returned to himself and sat for a long time pondering on these truths which are but a reiteration of Christ's own doctrine.

His musing found expression in self-reproach: "Look into the secret depths of your soul and you will see that, notwithstanding all your exterior penances, pride and self-love still rise in rebellion when you have to put up with a contradiction from others. You are like a scared rabbit hiding in a bush and trembling every time a leaf rustles in the breeze. This is how things stand with you: you shrink from sufferings which are not of your own seeking. The sight of uncongenial people makes you grow pale; you fly from humiliation, rejoice in praise, and avoid blame. Strike the iron while it is hot and enroll in the advanced school of holiness."[2]

Universities of the Spirit

This wonderful experience of Henry Suso in the "advanced school of holiness" speaks of the universities of the Spirit, instruction centers for our souls while our bodies sleep. At spiritual retreats located in the etheric plane, or heaven-world, our souls can systematically pursue the path of self-mastery under the ascended masters, angelic hosts and other heavenly beings. These retreats were once physical in various parts of the world, but they have since been withdrawn to higher levels.[3]

As an experiment in the twentieth century, the ascended masters have established a mystery school here at the Royal Teton Ranch in Montana. Their goal is to bring back into the physical octave the masters, their teachings and their path to union with God in order to give opportunity to all lightbearers of the world whose time has come to graduate from earth's schoolroom. Many spiritual seekers have a sense that this is the embodiment when they are to make their ascension, and they are drawn to these teachings and to our mystery school, to Summit University courses and quarterly retreats dedicated to communing with the masters. These retreats allow people from all walks of life and from all religious and spiritual backgrounds to gather together for a shared purpose—a greater realization of God.

Directions, Rebukes and Promises

The visions and locutions of the Christian mystics sometimes included specific directions, rebukes and promises. For example, Teresa of Avila said that one day Jesus commanded her to establish a new monastery. "He made great promises that it would be founded," she wrote, "and that He would be highly served in it. He said it should be called St. Joseph's."[4] As it turned out, a friend and patroness supplied the funds with which Teresa founded Saint Joseph's, a reformed Carmelite monastery.

On another occasion Jesus chided Teresa of Avila for failing to write down the insights he gave her. He said, "Don't neglect to write down what I say; for even though it may not benefit you, it can benefit others."[5]

You can develop a practice of writing down insights from Jesus, your spiritual mentor and your Holy Christ Self. Set aside a regular time for communion with God each day, even just fifteen minutes of meditation and spoken prayers. For many, the time just before they retire at night is ideal because there are no distractions.

Begin by expressing your gratitude. Also share your concerns and burdens. Pray for your soul to be tutored at the etheric retreats while your body sleeps (see pages 148-149). Leave your journal and a pen or pencil by your bedside so that upon awakening you can record the impressions, inspirations and instructions you recall. The answers you need may come quickly or they may take a while. Also record your dreams. Some dreams are symbolic, so ask your Holy Christ Self to decipher them and show you how to apply their lessons to your current circumstances.

Don't make a decision then and there that your impressions are absolutely correct and are the word of God, but write down what comes to you. Sift through the material. Discard that which is neither plausible nor rational. Act on what feels right to you and is consistent with what you know to be ethical and true. And then see what follows in your life. Let experience be the test of the accuracy of what you are hearing.

Free Will, Mistakes and Illumined Action

This next story, from Henry Suso's biography *The Exemplar*, illustrates what it means to give yourself to God.

On the following feast of the Assumption [of the Blessed Virgin] he was given another glimpse of heaven, but when he tried to enter, an angel stayed him with the words, "Sorry, Brother, but you will have to atone for your misdeeds before gaining admittance." Without further ado [the angel] led [Henry] over a twisted path to a dark cave, so narrow he could barely turn around. Left alone in this prison he spent the night grieving and bemoaning his pitiable condition. In the morning the angel returned and asked him how he felt.

"Awful, awful," sobbed [Henry].

"The Queen of Heaven is very irritated at your conduct," the angel said, "and that is why you are imprisoned here."

Startled by this information, [Henry] asked, "Poor me, and in what have I offended her Majesty?"

"You have repeatedly shown yourself unwilling to preach on her feastdays," the angel continued. "And yesterday, on the feast of her Assumption, you refused to preach even though your prior appointed you to do so."

"But, dear angel, it is because I consider myself unworthy of telling her praises and I feel that the older fathers could do far better than I, a poor wretch," [Henry] explained.

"Take my word for it," the angel reassured him, "that her Majesty prefers your halting words to the eloquence of your elders."

Half-choked with tears, [Henry] blurted out, "Dear angel, speak to her Majesty in my behalf, for I promise never again to falter in her praises."

The angel smiled, led [Henry] out of his prison, and on the homeward way told him, "Basing my statement on what her Majesty has told me about you, I tell you that she will receive you indulgently and show herself a gracious Mother."[6]

Now that we have heard the consequences for Henry Suso of avoiding his post, may we all be duly forewarned. Many individuals, when they are called to a particular service, make excuses as to why it would be better if someone else would do it, including the excuse that they are not so well tutored in their calling. But we don't need to be afraid to make mistakes. We have a right to make mistakes. Why else would God have given us free will? Free will is the grand and noble experiment whereby we achieve individuality in God. Everyone, including every student on the path to becoming God, has that right.

When an ascended master takes on a student, he anticipates that the student will make mistakes in the course of his discipleship. The student learns by his obedience to that master or by his own deliberations. Some deliberations will lead to right decisions and some may result in inaccurate conclusions, and so the student will make some mistakes and in this way he will learn.

Bishop William Connor Magee once said, "The man who makes no mistakes does not usually make anything."[7] So don't be afraid to make mistakes. It's not mistakes that cause you to fail. It's making the same mistake over and over again and not getting to the root of why you are doing it that can cause your failure and be your undoing. Danish inventor Piet Hein sums it up this way: "The road to wisdom? Well, it's plain and simple to express: Err, and err, and err again, but less, and less, and less."[8]

Adversity and the Dawn of Illumination

The writings of Columbus show that during his voyages of discovery in the West Indies he had profound mystical experiences that illustrate both the purgative and illuminative stages. They show the consolations that can come to the true mystic. It was on his return to Spain after discovering the New World that Columbus first heard the celestial voice which was to comfort him throughout his career. During his third voyage Columbus described this voice:

> The day after Christmas, 1499, after everyone had left me, I was attacked by Indians and ill-disposed Christians, and was placed in such an extremity that I had to flee for my life in a small caravel. Then the good Lord helped me, saying: "O man of a little faith, fear not, for I am with thee." And [the Lord] scattered my enemies and showed me how I might fulfil my vows.[9]

During his fourth voyage to the New World, Columbus was faced with unrelenting hardships. First he was caught in such a severe storm that he called it "a second Deluge.... Everything was worn out," he wrote, "ships and men alike.... My old wound opened, and for nine days I saw myself lost, without hope of life."[10]

He finally landed and repaired his ships as best he could but soon met again with contrary winds and currents. "The ships were no longer seaworthy, and the crews were mortally sick and exhausted," he wrote. His ships struggled to a safe harbor, but the men could not go ashore for a whole month because of unceasing rain. "I do not know whether any other man has suffered such torment," said Columbus.[11]

But his troubles did not stop there. The crew was short on provisions and they also encountered a waterspout, which Columbus said would have drowned them if they had not "broken it by

Christopher Columbus

reciting from the Gospel according to St. John."[12] Waterspouts are essentially tornadoes that occur over water. Heavily laden with air, spray and mist, they hang from a cloud like a column or funnel.

Columbus decided to leave eighty men behind to found a colony and to take the others back with him to Spain. But as he was departing, he heard the sounds of Indians attacking the men on shore. This continued for three hours while high winds and waves prevented him from going ashore to help them. That night he saw bodies floating toward him in the water. In this moment of despair, Columbus wrote to King Ferdinand and Queen Isabella:

> I was outside and all alone on this very dangerous coast, with a high fever and greatly exhausted. There was no hope of rescue. In this state, I climbed in pain to the highest point of the ship and called, in tears and trembling, to Your Highnesses' mighty men of war, in all the four corners of the earth, for succour, but none of them answered me.

At length, groaning with exhaustion, I fell asleep, and I heard a most merciful voice saying: "O fool, so slow to believe and to serve thy God, the God of all! What more did He do for Moses or for His servant David?

He has had thee in His care from thy mother's womb. When He saw thee a grown man, He caused thy name to resound most greatly over the earth. He gave thee the Indies, which are so rich a part of the world, and thou hast divided them according to thy desire. He gave thee the keys to the gates of the Ocean, which were held with such great chains.... Turn thyself to Him, and acknowledge thy sins. His mercy is infinite. Thine old age shall not prevent thee from achieving great things, for many and vast are His domains....

"Thou criest for help, with doubt in thy heart. Ask thyself who has afflicted thee so grievously and so often: God or the world? The privileges and covenants which God giveth are not taken back by Him.... Whatever He promises He fulfils with increase; for such are His ways. Thus have I told thee," [said the voice], "what thy Creator has done for thee, and for all men. He has now revealed to me some of those rewards which await thee for the many toils and dangers which thou hast endured in the service of others."

I heard all this as if in a trance, but I could find no reply to give to so sure a message, and all I could do was to weep over my transgressions. Whoever it was that had spoken, ended by saying: "Fear not, but have faith. All these tribulations are written upon tablets of marble, and there is reason for them."[13]

These are important words to remember when we face adversity, when we cannot comprehend how God would do such a thing to us, as Columbus had thought. "All these tribulations are written upon tablets of marble, and there is reason for them."

Truly, it is not God who does these things to us, but we who bring them upon ourselves. Adverse circumstances come to us either because our karma is returning to us or because God allows the world to test us, for we must also endure the persecutions of Christ. We must weather the storms of life and recognize that God has put us in his ship in this world and that he will see us to the other shore if we keep on striving, if we are not daunted by what anyone says about us or what anyone throws in our pathway.

Know who you are. Know what you are. Know that God lives in you. Take a stand for what you believe in and don't shy away from pursuing your life's mission. Walk in the footsteps of Christopher Columbus. Discover a new world for people, new dimensions of being. And once you make your discovery, make your charts and maps so clear that when you give them to others they will be able to enter that world because you have so clearly defined it in your meditations and in your communion with God.

The Voice that said "Fear not but have faith" was a voice of comfort and hope. It was a ray of illumination following the purgation of a dark night of the senses. This experience of Christopher Columbus is a hallmark in the annals of purgation and the dawn of illumination from God that followed it.

Prayers and Meditations

Blue-Lightning Protection

The color blue symbolizes the energy of protection. Archangel Michael and his angels most often appear dressed in blue-flame armour and surrounded by an intense blue and white light that looks like lightning.

As you give this decree to Archangel Michael, visualize yourself and your loved ones clothed in this blue-flame armour with light surrounding you. Throughout the day and before retiring at night, recall this image of Michael and his legions protecting you and others from physical dangers and harmful energies.

In the name of my mighty I AM Presence and Holy Christ Self, I decree for the protection of myself, my loved ones, and all children of God:

> *Blue lightning is thy love,*
> *Flood forth to free all;*
> *Blue lightning is thy power,*
> *In God I see all;*
> *Blue lightning is thy mind,*
> *In pure truth I find*
>
> *Light will overcome,*
> *Light will make us one.*
> *Light from blue-fire sun,*
> *Command us now all free!*
>
> *Blue lightning is thy Law,*
> *Blaze forth as holy awe;*
> *Blue lightning is thy name,*
> *Our heart's altar do enflame;*

Blue lightning maketh free,
In God I'll ever be.

Light will overcome
Light will make us one
Light from blue-fire sun
Command us now all free!

And in full Faith I consciously accept this manifest,
manifest, manifest! (3x) right here and now with full
Power, eternally sustained, all-powerfully active, ever ex-
panding and world enfolding until all are wholly ascended
in the light and free! Beloved I AM! Beloved I AM!
Beloved I AM!

Prayer for Soul Journey
to the Universities of the Spirit

Tens of thousands of souls journey to the universities of the Spirit in their finer bodies while their physical bodies sleep. Here they are tutored in many areas of knowledge—spiritual teachings and the profound truths of all religions; the science of healing, mathematics, music, the laws of alchemy and precipitation; understanding the intricacies of the will of God in politics, religion, business, finance and education; and other areas. Various courses provide tutoring in subjects like gaining mastery of the emotions and quieting inordinate desire, invoking light for dealing with karma, and anchoring etheric patterns in tangible ways to improve everyday life—patterns of self-reliance in God, the sacred family and God-government.

Before going to sleep, say the following prayer or one of your own. Call to Archangel Michael and your Holy Christ Self for protection and ask that your soul be escorted on her journey to and from the spiritual retreats:

Beloved Holy Christ Self, Archangel Michael and angels of light, I ask that you take me in my soul consciousness to the universities of the Spirit. Escort me, instruct me, guide and protect me. I ask to be filled and inspired with the will of God and tutored in _____ [make your personal requests here].

I ask that all information necessary for the fulfillment of my divine plan be released to my outer waking consciousness as it is required. I thank you and I accept it done this hour in full power.

Your conscious mind won't necessarily remember everything you have learned at these universities of the Spirit, but the information may come to you as inspiration and flashes of insight.

CHAPTER 11

Illumination through Revelation

any Christian mystics have experienced God as light or fire. One of Catherine of Siena's prayers reads: "In your nature, eternal Godhead, I shall come to know my nature. And what is my nature...? It is fire, because you are nothing but a fire of love. And you have given human-kind a share in this nature, for by the fire of love you created us."[1]

Oftentimes the mystics have perceived the Divine as a dazzling, blinding light. For some, the divine radiance appeared at times to shine through their physical form. Bonaventure reported that on one occasion Saint Francis' whole body was "wrapped in a shining cloud."[2]

Henry Suso also experienced God as light. His biog-raphy describes how one night "he became absorbed in contemplation and it seemed to him that the sun was try-ing to escape from the prison of his heart. He tore open his tunic and saw that his breast was flooded with radiance and surmounted with a gold cross imbedded with precious, glistening stones."[3]

Teresa of Avila was aware of being surrounded by a tube of light. She said, "I saw a large multitude of devils around me, and it seemed that a great brightness encircled me, and this prevented them from reaching me. I understood that God was watching over me so that they could not get to me in order to make me offend Him."[4]

Meister Eckhart gave this teaching about the aura of those who are fused with God:

> He...who has abandoned himself and all that is his will be truly and utterly fused with God. Wherever you touched him you would come upon God, for he is wholly in God, and God surrounds him as my cowl surrounds my head, and whosoever would touch me would first have to touch my gown. And similarly, when I drink, the draught must first pass over my tongue, for there the draught is tasted. When the tongue is coated with bitterness, no matter how sweet the wine may be, it must grow bitter through what it must pass to reach me....
>
> So he who has completely abandoned his own self would be so completely surrounded with God that nothing created could touch him without first touching upon God. And whatever was to reach him would have to pass God first, and there it would get its savour and grow divine. No matter how great a sorrow may be, if it comes by way of God, God has already suffered it.
>
> Contempt becomes honour, the bitter grows sweet, and deepest darkness turns to clearest light. Everything takes on the savour of God and becomes divine. For whatever befalls such a man [whose aura is fused with God] is shaped for him in God; he thinks nothing else and feels nothing else, and thus he experiences God in all bitterness as well as in supreme ecstasy.[5]

The mystics have never seen human happiness as the goal of life. Rather, they view human happiness and human suffering as instruments that can be used to propel the soul Godward. They look at life from the standpoint of the soul and concern themselves with tutoring the soul, assisting her to balance karma, and bringing her ever closer to God.

Many wonder why it is that God allows suffering. From the standpoint of the spiritual path, bearing an affliction does not prevent an individual from making spiritual progress, and in some cases having an affliction helps a soul to make progress. Think about the many saints who have borne serious ailments in their body. Bearing their own karma or a portion of the sins of the world in this manner may have humbled them, preventing them from being puffed up with pride and idolatry of the outer form. And so, instead of striving for the perfectionment of the body temple, they transformed it into a chalice in which to contain the light of Christ.

Transfiguration by the Divine Light

Author Sidney Spencer noted that for the mystics of the Eastern Orthodox Church, the experience of God "comes typically as a vision of the divine Light, which transforms and deifies the soul [that is, it makes the soul one with God]." Spencer reported:

> [Saint Symeon] tells of a young man who received a vision of the Light.... While he was at prayer, "a brilliant divine radiance descended on him from above, and filled all the room. Thereupon the young man forgot that he was in a room or beneath a roof, for on all sides he saw nothing but light.... Love and the cleaving of his heart to God brought him into ecstasy, and transformed him wholly into the Light of the Holy Spirit."
>
> The divine Light which the mystics saw was identified in their interpretation with the Glory of God which appeared in...the Old Testament (as Moses' vision of the Burning Bush) and which was

Saint Symeon

revealed to the three disciples of Jesus at the Transfiguration and to St. Paul on the road to Damascus.

Particular emphasis was laid on the Transfiguration.... The mystics sought to identify themselves with Christ in his divine glory.... Again and again Eastern saints have felt themselves to be transfigured by the divine Light which shone through Jesus....

[Saint Symeon] himself declares: "I am filled with light and glory; my face shines like that of my Beloved, and all my members glow with heavenly Light."[6]

Chiseling the Image of Christhood

Among the most striking illuminations given to the Christian mystics were revelations about Jesus. The mystics have seen Christ in many roles, including teacher, guide, saviour, intercessor, mother and bridegroom. Christ appeared to the seventeenth-century Peruvian saint Rose of Lima as a sculptor who taught her a very important lesson. John Arintero tells the story:

Shortly after St. Rose of Lima had been clothed in the Dominican habit, our Lord showed her...a marvelous vision. He presented Himself to her to be espoused with her, but He came in the guise of a sculptor and He charged her to fashion certain blocks of marble. Since she was not able to perform such an arduous task, she excused herself to Him by saying that she knew very well how to sew and spin, but to sculpture stones, she was not able.

"Do you think," Christ asked her, "that you are the only one who is commanded to occupy yourself in such rude labor?"

Then He showed her an immense workshop where a great multitude of young women was employed at the same task. With great ease and zeal they were wielding, not a needle, but a chisel and hammer. That their work might be accelerated that their stones might come forth more brilliant, they watered them with many tears. Some of the stones were yet to be finished, but others were sculptured with such finesse and delicacy that not the slightest defect could be seen in them. In the midst of such lowly labor the young women were decked out in their best finery but, instead of being soiled with dust, they were resplendent with supernatural beauty.[7]

Jesus was showing Rose of Lima that we are all called to chisel the image of our own Christhood. Arintero reflects:

We are those hard stones, filled with impurities and roughness, which must be worked and polished with great care. All of us are called to the same task of working and watering with our sweat and tears this unpolished stone of our nature in order to change it into a masterpiece in which the image of Jesus Christ shines forth perfectly.[8]

In courses at the etheric retreats, modern mystics strive to re-move flaws and rough spots in their human nature in preparation

Saint Rose of Lima, *by Claudio Coello*

for their soul's alchemical union with her Lord. At one retreat, students are assigned in groups of five or more to carry out projects with others whose karmic patterns forecast the maximum friction between them. This is done in order to test their spiritual mettle and determination to be centered in God. Each group stays together until the members become harmonious, individually and as a cohesive unit. Through this process they often learn that the character traits they find most offensive in others are the polar opposite of their own worst faults and that what one criticizes in another is apt to be the root of his own misery.

When souls who have been placed in close proximity precisely because they have rubbed each other the wrong way for lifetimes have succeeded in smoothing their rough places and achieving God-harmony, they can move on to progressively more advanced courses that in time will result in the soul's alchemical marriage to her Holy Christ Self and in her ultimate union with her I AM Presence in the ritual of the ascension.

Jesus as Intercessor

In another vision, Jesus appeared to Rose of Lima as the Intercessor:

> In the hands of the Lord, I saw a great scales, with balances and squadrons of angels, illustrious with festive ornament, who bowed before the Divine Majesty.... The Angels, taking the balances, began to load afflictions.... Christ intervened and took upon Himself the office of arbiter. He made the scales true, and from the piles upon the balances distributed afflictions to the souls present there, setting aside for me a heavy portion of adversity.
>
> Afterwards, placing new weights upon the balances, blessings were heaped upon blessings, and as the angels leaned to read the weight Christ intervened again, His omnipotent arm alone being equal to the task. He marked it exactly, and with great attention divided among the souls as many blessings as He had given them afflictions. To your handmaid He distributed inestimable riches. This done, the Saviour raised His voice and said with majesty: "Know that the grace corresponds to tribulation. This is the one true Scales of Paradise."
>
> And when I heard Him speak I longed to rush out into the plaza and tell all people the truth. My soul almost left my body in its eager ardour.... For no one would cry out against his heavy cross if he knew the balances on which it has been weighed.[9]

In Rose of Lima's vision, Jesus didn't take away afflictions; he balanced them with blessings. This is consistent with his promise on the occasion when Peter asked him: "We have forsaken all, and followed thee; what shall we have therefore?"[10] Jesus responded:

> Verily I say unto you, There is no man that hath left house, or brethren, or sisters, or father, or mother, or wife, or children, or lands, for my sake, and the gospel's, but he shall receive an

hundredfold now in this time, houses, and brethren, and sisters, and mothers, and children, and lands, with persecutions; and in the world to come eternal life. But many that are first shall be last; and the last first.[11]

When a soul gives herself to God, God gives that soul much grace in return. Many have given up everything in the service of God and discovered that everything Jesus promised has been fulfilled, including persecutions. It is the role of the living Christ to adjudicate karma. He gives the soul afflictions, which are her negative karma returning, as well as blessings, her positive karma. In addition, he gives his grace so that the soul can be strengthened to pass her tests.

In his role as Saviour, Jesus saves our souls to work out our own salvation. He teaches us how to carry our cross of karma even as he carries it for us. And then, when we are strengthened and infilled with the sacred fire, he gives that karma back to us to give to us our dignity as sons and daughters of God, that we might have the dignity of bearing our own weight. Once we understand this, we wouldn't have it any other way.

Jesus as Mother

One of the most interesting insights in Christian mysticism is the portrayal of Jesus as Mother. The fourteenth-century English mystic Julian of Norwich recorded some of the most unique mystical revelations about the motherhood of Jesus Christ. "As truly as God is our Father," she wrote, "so truly is God our Mother."[12]

Even before Julian's day, the concept of God as Mother was not new to the Judeo-Christian tradition. In the Old Testament and the Apocrypha, Wisdom is personified as female.

The Gospel of Matthew records that Jesus applied the image

of mother to himself when he lamented over Jerusalem and likened himself to a hen that gathereth her chicks under her wings. Our Lord noted that he was not received by the people of his time as the Divine Mother. He looked over the city from a high place and cried out:

> O Jerusalem, Jerusalem, thou that killest the prophets, and stonest them which are sent unto thee, how often would I have gathered thy children together, even as a hen gathereth her chicks under her wings, and ye would not![13]

They would not receive Jesus as the Divine Word, the Word that is Feminine in God. And so today we have another round and another opportunity to receive Jesus—not only as our brother but also as our mother.

In the eleventh century, Saint Anselm compared Christ to a nursemaid to the faithful and addressed a prayer to Jesus: "In truth, Lord, you are my Mother."[14] In Saint Catherine of Siena's *Dialogue*, God the Father said that the soul becoming one with Christ is like an infant who "rests on its mother's breast, takes her nipple, and drinks her milk through her flesh.... The soul rests on the breast of Christ crucified...and so drinks in the milk of virtue."[15]

Julian of Norwich went a step further than her predecessors and developed a theology around the motherhood of Christ. Christ, she realized, gives us not only birth but re-birth. Julian said that "God almighty is our loving Father," "God all wisdom is our loving Mother," and God as the Holy Spirit provides love and goodness. She called the second Person of the Trinity, the Son, "our Mother in nature" and "our Mother of mercy."[16] She explained:

> In our Mother of mercy, we have our reforming and our restoring.... The kind, loving mother who knows and sees the need of her

child guards it very tenderly.... And always as the child grows in age and in stature, she acts differently, but she does not change her love. And when it is even older, she allows it to be chastised to destroy its faults, so as to make the child receive virtues and grace.

This work...our Lord performs in those by whom it is done.... In our spiritual bringing to birth he uses more tenderness, without any comparison, in protecting us.... He kindles our understanding, he prepares our ways, he eases our conscience, he comforts our soul, he illumines our heart.... And when we fall, quickly he raises us up with his loving embrace and his gracious touch.[17]

Prayers and Meditations

Tube of Light Decree

Note the striking similarity between the wording of the "Tube of Light Decree" below and Teresa of Avila's description of the "great brightness" that encircled her and protected her. This short decree, given daily, can protect you from discord:

> *Beloved I AM Presence bright,*
> *Round me seal your tube of light*
> *From ascended master flame*
> *Called forth now in God's own name.*
> *Let it keep my temple free*
> *From all discord sent to me.*
>
> *I AM calling forth violet fire*
> *To blaze and transmute all desire,*
> *Keeping on in freedom's name*
> *Till I AM one with the violet flame.*

Transfiguration Decree

Here too, note the parallels between the imagery in the "Transfiguration Decree" and in the vision of the young man who was "transformed...wholly into the Light of the Holy Spirit."

> *I AM changing all my garments,*
> *Old ones for the bright new day;*
> *With the sun of understanding*
> *I AM shining all the way.*

I AM light within, without;
I AM light is all about.
Fill me, free me, glorify me!
Seal me, heal me, purify me!
Until transfigured they describe me:
I AM shining like the Son,
I AM shining like the sun!

"Thy Kingdom Come"—The Prayer of the Christ

This is the prayer of the Christ in Jesus and in you. With it you are affirming that the patterns on earth shall be established after the patterns in heaven and that only God's will shall be done on earth and in your life. You are exercising the authority God has given you to command spiritual and material resources in his name.

Our Father, may thy kingdom come now into manifestation. May the senseless delays and frustrations imposed by ignorance and the spirit of vain competition be stayed; for these have separated brother from brother and splintered the wholly innocent thought of faith—the divine credo—into manifold arrows of mortal hostility.

Gather thou from every corner of the earth and from the four corners of the heavens the spirits of just men made perfect by love; and let their daily offerings and sacrifices flow forth now as pure light energy to bless thy infinite habitation. For they are also born of thy radiant crystal fire mist, which mirrors in part the stream of thy invisible radiance and renders the invisible Holy One visible unto thy children.

May thy luminous essence draw all men unto thee and thy supreme purpose, that thy coming kingdom may be made a reality by the many hands offered in supplicant service to thy holy cause, by the many hearts beating in unison with thine own, and by the many minds perceiving the paradise creation reappearing from the secret place of the Most High.

For it is thy love which beareth fruit in the garden of men's souls and leadeth them gently by the hand through the straight and narrow gate of thy kingdom of infinite expansion, where the artificial senses and defenses of humankind melt in the sunburst of thy light and dawning illumination.

Let brotherhood, peace and progress become landmarks of attainment. Let unity of purpose be assured and let the cities of this earth become cities of God. Let the planet earth, which thou hast drenched with thy rains of divine mercy and showered upon with the bounties of thy harvest of spiritual grace, be raised now to the height of God-attainment. Gather thou the souls of men into thy kingdom through thy holy seasons and cycles of manifestation.

Two thousand years ago I sat upon my Mother's knee and felt her holy innocence flowing into my soul, reestablishing the matrix of the Motherhood of God even as thou expressed in thy ever-near Presence, revealing thyself unto me as my heavenly Father. Be thou the All-in-all to all men. Let every child of thy heart drink deeply of the draft of immortality.

Let the great seed of thy Word, thou sower of expanding souls, be disseminated anew upon the fields of the world. Let the Holy Spirit touch all with the light upon the mount—yea, upon the summit of attainment. Let freedom be cast abroad and honored upon thy altars and let liberty waft upon every breeze the sweet air of divine inheritance.

Thy kingdom come! Thy victory be established! Thy way be made plain! Let thy deliverance to the family of nations come forth now! We decree it so; and thou, O LORD, shall establish it from generation unto generation henceforth and forevermore.

Union

CHAPTER 12

Spiritual Betrothal

ven with its moments of bliss, the illuminative stage is
merely a foretaste of the splendid and perpetual union
with God that comes in the unitive stage. The mystics tell
us that the soul's union with God in this life should be the
goal of all Christians. They have referred to this union as
the spiritual marriage, the deifying, transforming union,
or deification. This concept of the soul's deification has a
history in early Christian tradition.

Many of the mystics experienced the soul to be feminine in nature and the intended bride of Christ. Before the
spiritual marriage can take place, however, the soul passes
through a period of a betrothal, or engagement. Teresa of
Avila explained that in the spiritual betrothal the soul and
the Beloved "are frequently separated" and the soul is
deprived of the Lord's constant companionship. But in
the marriage union, "the soul remains all the time...with
its God."[1]

During the spiritual betrothal the soul undergoes further tests and purgations in preparation for her marriage

to Christ, but she also enjoys the delights of God. The mystics have described the mystical engagement in varying ways and as containing different elements and emphasis. In the process of perfecting the soul, God gives the soul what she needs.

As you read these descriptions of what the mystics experienced during their spiritual betrothal, you will see echoed certain aspects of the purgative and illuminative stages, and indeed they are further refinements of the process of emptying the soul of all that is not God.

Love Initiations of the Mystics

The Christian mystics spoke candidly about spiritual union and the love initiations that precede and accompany it. Saint Thérèse of Lisieux said that from the age of fourteen she experienced "assaults of love" that consumed her like a "veritable flame."[2] She wrote:

> I was in the choir...when I felt myself suddenly wounded by a dart of fire so ardent that I thought I should die.... There is no comparison to describe the intensity of that flame. It seemed as though an invisible force plunged me wholly into fire.... But oh! what fire! what sweetness![3]

So enflamed was she by a love that is beyond this world that she wrote in her autobiography, "O Jesus,...my *vocation*, at last I have found it.... *My vocation is love!*"[4]

One of the most famous encounters recorded in mystical literature is what is called the ecstasy of Saint Teresa of Avila. In a vision, the Lord showed Teresa a small angel holding a large golden dart tipped with fire. She said:

> It seemed to me this angel plunged the dart several times into my heart.... When he drew [the dart] out, I thought he was carrying off with him the deepest part of me; and he left me all on fire with great love of God.[5]

The Ecstasy of Saint Teresa, *by Bernini*

Jesus told Catherine of Genoa that these flaming darts "of an irresistible love" are like "waves of fire.... They flow from My breast," Jesus said, "and communicate such ardor and interior power to man that he can now do nothing else but love, remaining inseparably united with his God."[6]

Unable to adequately express the overwhelming love she felt for God, Catherine of Genoa simply said: "If [one drop] of that love my heart feels...were to fall into Hell, Hell itself would altogether turn into Eternal life."[7]

Isn't this the love we all seek? The love that will heal, the love that with one single drop will transform someone's world. Just think what we could do if we had that kind of love! But in order to have that kind of love, we need to open our hearts all the way. And as we know, it is not always easy to do that. Because of the wounds of the past, we close up when loving gets too painful. We sometimes have to contact deep levels of hurt in order to resolve the painful record and move on.

The Living Flame of Love

Saint John of the Cross spoke of the love shared by the bride and her divine Spouse as the "living flame of love." He used the metaphor of a log enkindled with this flame to describe the mystical union he experienced:

> With time and practice, love can receive added quality...and become more intensified. We have an example of this in the activity of fire: Although the fire has penetrated the wood, transformed it, and united it with itself, yet as this fire grows hotter and continues to burn, the wood becomes much more incandescent and inflamed, even to the point of flaring up and shooting out flames from itself.
>
> It should be understood that the soul now speaking has reached this enkindled degree, and is so inwardly transformed in the fire of love and has received such quality from it that it is not merely united to this fire but produces within it a living flame....
>
> And that flame, every time it flares up, bathes the soul in glory and refreshes it with the quality of divine life.... We can compare the soul...in this state of transformation of love to the log of wood that is ever immersed in fire, and the acts of this soul to the flame that blazes up from the fire of love. The more intense the fire of union, the more vehemently does this fire burst into flames.[8]

Saint John was speaking from intimate experience with the living flame of love. He experienced God as love and he was transformed by God through a life lived in perfect, selfless love. This transformation of our souls through the fire of love is what Jesus and the saints and masters convey when they come to us. They come to ignite the fire in our hearts and to help us become a fire that can ignite other hearts.

Francis of Assisi receiving the stigmata, fresco by Giotto

The mystical wounds of love are sometimes physically visible on the body as the stigmata, marks resembling Jesus' crucifixion wounds. Saint Francis of Assisi, who lived in the thirteenth century, is the first person known to have received the stigmata. Since then there have been over three hundred known authentic stigmatists, including, in the twentieth century, Therese Neumann and Padre Pio. Miraculously, the physical body of a number of stigmatists was restored after their death to the appearance of youth and beauty, including Saint Francis of Assisi, Saint Catherine of Siena, Saint Magdalen of Pazzi and Saint Rose of Lima.

Catherine of Siena understood the true meaning of imitating the life of Christ, and in 1375 she received the stigmata. At first the wounds were visible to others. But Catherine, preferring to share Christ's passion in secret, prayed in humility that they might be made invisible. God answered her prayer, and afterwards she alone was able to see them. Nonetheless she continued to suffer the pain of the stigmata, and this allowed her to bear a portion of the cross of world karma.

Self-Emptying

Johannes Tauler said in one of his sermons: "In the same measure that a man comes out from himself, in that measure does God enter in with His divine grace."[9] This is the great mystery that the mystics of all religions have unlocked: In order to be full, you must first be empty. In order for God to dwell in you completely, you must first empty yourself of all that is not God.

I counsel many people regarding their absence of a sense of self-worth, their self-image, and their sense of not having worth in the sight of God. This condition is very understandable when a person has had a glorious vision of the I AM THAT I AM. He sees God and himself beside God, and he naturally thinks of the lost time and energy, the byways he has taken, the burdens and sins. For someone who has had this experience, it is normal to compare what he can be with what he is at present.

So if we have an experience like this and then someone comes along and tells us that we not a terrible person but a wonderful person, it almost interferes with the very process whereby God allows us to look at our lesser self. God wants us to look at the records of our karma and the doings of our carnal mind. He brings to our remembrance all of the things that we could possibly have done to offend life in this and other incarnations. This is because we have to see and purge, relent from wrongdoing, overcome and put behind us all these things. What we have been, we must acknowledge. And what we have been, as we can truly see, has at times not been the beauty of our own Christhood.

In this hour and in this day we are called to come up higher. Jesus and Saint Germain have given us the violet flame. As we invoke the flame with intensity, we will see much passing into it. And yet, although much karmic substance can pass into the flame, these offenses will not disappear automatically. We still have to learn the

lesson God wants us to understand. And when we do, then we can
come up higher. What a tremendous gift of grace God has given us
in the opportunity we have to attain reunion with the living Christ
and to have our threefold flame intensified and exalted!

The Dark Night of the Spirit

Prior to the spiritual marriage the soul passes through what
Saint John of the Cross refers to as the dark night of the Spirit.
This is an advanced initiation that comes to the soul only when
she has internalized a certain level of Christhood. Saint John said
that during this period the soul feels that "God has abandoned it,
and, in His abhorrence of it, has flung it into darkness." The soul
feels "chastised and cast out, and unworthy of Him." "It feels, too,
that all creatures have forsaken it, and that it is condemned by
them, particularly by its friends."[10]

Saint John described the dark night of the Spirit as an "inflow
of God into the soul."[11] With this infusion of Spirit, God is

purging the soul, annihilating it, emptying it or consuming in it
(even as fire consumes the mouldiness and the rust of metal) all the
affections and imperfect habits which it has contracted in its whole
life.... God greatly humbles the soul in order that He may afterwards greatly exalt it.[12]

This is a wondrous understanding of the dark night of the
Spirit. Not one of us shall ever be exempt from this path. We shall
all go through it. When the dark night of the senses or the dark
night of the Spirit comes upon us, it will be a total blackness. And
all we will have to go on is the Christ we have already realized in
our heart, our own burning love for the Saviour, our own absolute
faith and trust that God will see us through and we will get to the
other side of the darkness and the blackness.

Saint John of the Cross and Teresa of Avila came along when there were no priests or prelates to actually counsel the many sisters and brothers who were following a mystical path and who did not understand the steps and the stages of moving toward the living flame of love and yet having this flame reject them, of desiring to enter into the secret chamber of the heart and yet being rebuffed by the Holy Christ Self and by Jesus, who say, "Go back and complete that fiery trial and that testing and that purging; you are not yet prepared to be my bride." And so these saints wrote of their experiences in order to leave a detailed road map for others to follow.

The dark night of the Spirit, then, must come to all. Therefore, welcome it. Prepare for it. And get through it as quickly as God will allow you to do, as quickly as you know how to do, by applying the teachings of the mystics who have walked this path before you.

The Supreme Test

The culmination of the dark night of the Spirit is the initiation of the crucifixion. What part of us is crucified in the crucifixion? It is not the outer self; it is the Christ who is embodied in us. Jesus the Christ was crucified. Had he not been the Christ, they would not have bothered crucifying him.

Insofar as we allow Christ to be formed in us and to intensify and intensify, insofar as we have the courage to be a Christ and to want Christ so much that we do not care what the world does to us or with us, we will come to that place of the crucifixion. And with the ascended masters' teachings, we can prepare for that initiation and pass it.

The crucifixion is the supreme test of individual Christhood when the soul is, as it were, cut off from the I AM Presence and must survive in spiritual consciousness solely on the God-energy, on the Christ-energy, that she has mastered and internalized in all lifetimes on the Path. She must be able to sustain that internalized God Presence where she is while holding the balance for planetary karma without reinforcement from the I AM Presence above.

This is the initiation that Jesus underwent on the cross. Mark Prophet used to speak of this initiation often in his lectures. And he said this is the real explanation of why Jesus suddenly cried out from the cross, "My God, my God, why hast thou forsaken me?"[13]

The meaning of that highest and most difficult initiation that we must pass before we can come to the resurrection is this: We must have internalized the Word that we are—an individual identity in God that is self-sustaining. And when we have passed that test, we will also be one with our I AM Presence.

Knowing God Directly as the Self

To attain union with God takes belief in God's being. We cannot reach the Divine through the intellect, the emotions, the imagination or any of the senses. With these we build bridges to God. We think of concepts. We imagine pathways. We think of this, that and the next thing. Rituals and exercises are necessary at a certain point. But when we come to the dark night of the Spirit, anything that is a means to an end is also a means of separation from that end. In other words: I am here, God is there. I need my intellect, my imagination, my senses, et cetera, to get to him. If I have none of these, I also eliminate time and space; and my love of God is of God in me, and there is no longer any separation.

To be willing to undergo this, to be willing to know and perceive God directly as the Self, takes great courage. It means to have experience in the spherical body and the spherical consciousness, to be willing to walk away from all of the previous modes of finding God. This is the practice of the contemplatives who still all the senses—the eyes, the ears, the mouth. They close themselves to everything external in order to find God. The question is, do we love God enough to throw out all the established means, all that we have been programmed and educated to use to attain a reasonable equilibrium in this life?

The great theme in the life of Saint Clare of Assisi was to empty herself that God might fill her. To her, the vow of poverty was for the creation of a vacuum that God could then fill. To be totally impoverished is to be "the poor in spirit," who shall inherit "the kingdom of heaven." By being in possession of nothing, we create the vacuum that nature abhors. And Nature, as God, fills that vacuum.

If our mind is filled with the memories of the things of this world that we have or desire to possess, it's like having a full attic. We seek, rather, to be filled with hope and only hope, our souls waiting upon the coming of the Lord. The Holy Spirit illumines such souls.

So it is through the purging that comes with the dark night of the Spirit that the soul is at last ready to enter into the bridal chamber.

Prayers and Meditations

It is Finished!

The Gospel of John records that the last words of Jesus on the cross were, "It is finished."[14] These words were not alone for Jesus. When we give the prayer "It Is Finished!" we are declaring that we are finished with the round of making karma and with the entanglements of the world. We are taking our stand and affirming our identity with Christ today.

"It is finished" is an affirmation that the human consciousness, with all of its struggles, crucifixions and trials, is finished. We are engaged in an ongoing process of God-mastery, and each time we affirm "It is finished," we are taking a scientific action with God. It is not a one-time event; we are being reborn daily. We have old habit patterns and our energies tend to fall into those patterns and outpicture them in the same way. So if we want change, we renew ourselves daily. With Paul, we die daily and we are daily being reborn at a higher level of consciousness.

As you give the following affirmation, visualize yourself in the hour of your victory, the point of your soul's readiness for the alchemical marriage—your soul's union, or spiritual marriage, with her Beloved, your Holy Christ Self, and with Christ Jesus:

> *It is finished!*
> *Done with this episode in strife,*
> *I AM made one with immortal life.*
> *Calmly I AM resurrecting my spiritual energies*
> *From the great treasure-house of immortal knowing.*
> *The days I knew with thee, O Father,*
> *Before the world was—the days of triumph,*
> *When all of the thoughts of thy Being*

Soared over the ageless hills of cosmic memory;
Come again as I meditate upon thee.
Each day as I call forth thy memories
From the scroll of immortal love,
I AM thrilled anew.
Patterns wondrous to behold enthrall me
With the wisdom of thy creative scheme.
So fearfully and wonderfully am I made
That none can mar thy design,
None can despoil the beauty of thy holiness,
None can discourage the beating of my heart
In almost wild anticipation
Of thy fullness made manifest within me.

O great and glorious Father,
How shall a tiny bird created in hierarchical bliss
Elude thy compassionate attention?
I AM of greater value than many birds
And therefore do I know that thy loving thoughts
Reach out to me each day
To console me in seeming aloneness,
To raise my courage,
Elevate my concepts,
Exalt my character,
Flood my being with virtue and power,
Sustain thy cup of life flowing over within me,
And abide within me forever
In the nearness of thy heavenly Presence.

I cannot fail,
Because I AM thyself in action everywhere.
I ride with thee

Upon the mantle of the clouds.
I walk with thee
Upon the waves and crests of water's abundance.
I move with thee
In the undulations of thy currents
Passing over the thousands of hills
 composing earth's crust.
I AM alive with thee
In each bush, flower, and blade of grass.
All nature sings in thee and me,
For we are one.
I AM alive in the hearts of the downtrodden,
Raising them up.
I AM the Law exacting the truth of being
In the hearts of the proud,
Debasing the human creation therein
And spurring the search for thy Reality.
I AM all things of bliss
To all people of peace.
I AM the full facility of divine grace,
The Spirit of Holiness
Releasing all hearts from bondage into unity.

It is finished!
Thy perfect creation is within me.
Immortally lovely,
It cannot be denied the blessedness of being.
Like unto thyself, it abides in the house of Reality.
Nevermore to go out into profanity,
It knows only the wonders of purity and victory.
Yet there stirs within this immortal fire
A consummate pattern of mercy and compassion

Seeking to save forever that which is lost
Through wandering away
From the beauty of Reality and Truth.
I AM the living Christ in action evermore!

It is finished!
Death and human concepts have no power in my world!
I AM sealed by God-design
With the fullness of that Christ-love
That overcomes, transcends, and frees the world
By the power of the three-times-three
Until all the world is God-victorious—
Ascended in the light and free!

It is finished!
Completeness is the allness of God.
Day unto day an increase of strength, devotion,
Life, beauty, and holiness occurs within me,
Released from the fairest flower of my being,
The Christ-consecrated rose of Sharon
Unfolding its petals within my heart.
My heart is the heart of God!
My heart is the heart of the world!
My heart is the heart of Christ in healing action!
Lo, I AM with you alway, even unto the end,
When with the voice of immortal love
I, too, shall say, "It is finished!"

CHAPTER 13

The Soul's Spiritual Marriage to Christ

he mystics' description of their love pact with the Beloved has produced some of the most exalted expressions of love ever written. Saint John of the Cross wrote of the personal and intimate contact of his soul with the Divine One:

> All things I then forgot,
> My cheek on him who for my coming came;
> All ceased, and I was not,
> Leaving my cares and shame
> Among the lilies, and forgetting them.[1]

The spiritual marriage is not simply a conforming to the ways and will of God but a total transforming of the soul into God. These are not my words. This is precisely how the mystics describe the divine union. Saint John wrote: "[When] the soul is...carried away and absorbed in love, [it is] as if she had vanished and been dissolved in love...passing out of self to the Beloved."[2]

This is the very heart of the teaching that is only whispered: The soul that is transformed into God *is God*.

This is the conclusion the mystics inevitably reached, but they were often reluctant to tell it, for they feared persecution.

The apostle Paul was speaking of the path to union with Christ when he said, "I am crucified with Christ: nevertheless I live; yet not I, but Christ liveth in me."[3] When Christ lives in us we can say with Paul that we do not live (that is, our lesser self no longer lives), because when Christ lives fully in us we have become one with that Christ and there's no longer any difference between us—between our soul and our Holy Christ Self. The bonding has taken place.

This is the meaning of walking the earth as a Christed, or anointed, one. Your Holy Christ Self is no longer above you, as it appears in the Chart of Your Divine Self (opposite page 34); it has descended to occupy your form. Those who are one with Christ experience all of his passions, all of his life. When you have been willing to be crucified with Jesus, no longer are there two, but only one.

United Indissolubly with God

John Arintero says that in the unitive stage

the soul, indissolubly united and made one with the incarnate Word, vividly bears His divine image and seems to be Jesus Christ Himself...living on earth.[4]

Saint Francis of Assisi, for example, so dedicated himself to the imitation of Christ that he was called "another Christ."[5] In the act of union, said Tauler, there is "nothing in the soul beside God."[6]

Teresa of Avila said the union of the soul with God is

like rain falling from the heavens into a river or a spring; there is nothing but water there and it is impossible to divide or separate the water belonging to the river from that which fell from the heavens. Or it is as if...in a room there were two large windows through which the light streamed in: it enters in different places but it all becomes one.[7]

The Spanish mystic Luis de León said that when the soul is united with God, it "not only has God dwelling within it, but is indeed God."[8]

Saint Magdalen of Pazzi, a sixteenth-century mystic, cried out to the Father:

> By means of the union and transformation of Thyself into the soul and of the soul into Thee,...Thou dost deify the soul. O deification! The soul which has the happiness of arriving at the state of being made God, like a sphere irradiating the rays of the sun, is made luminous and resplendent as the sun itself. We are transformed into Thy very image, from clarity to clarity.[9]

These are the words of the Christian mystics and the teachings of the Doctors and Fathers of the Church. The goal of deification— becoming one with God or, as some of the mystics say, *becoming God*—has been a part of the Christian mystical tradition since the time of Jesus Christ.

The mystics have described their spiritual marriage with Christ very graphically. In 1730 Father Bernard Hoyos heard angels singing, "Behold, the Bridegroom is coming, go forth to meet Him." In a vision he saw Jesus, the Blessed Mother, and many saints. He heard Jesus say: "I espouse thee, O beloved soul, in an eternal espousal of love.... Now thou art Mine and I am thine.... Thou art Bernard of Jesus and I am Jesus of Bernard.... Thou and I are one."[10]

Commentators on the Christian mystics note that male mystics whom Christ espouses sometimes experience Christ as Wisdom or Mercy because these are considered to be feminine attributes of God. Jacob Boehme, for instance, spoke of the soul's marriage to the Virgin Sophia, meaning Wisdom.

The Marriage of St. Catherine, *by Pierre Subleyras*

The most important assignment we have in this life is to pursue our soul's bonding to Jesus Christ and through him the bonding to our Holy Christ Self whereby, through this fusion, we are nevermore separated from the living Christ.

This union must take place because a long, long time ago we had that bonding and we allowed the serpents and the fallen angels to pry us from our Lord. And so we lost that bonding and some people lost the threefold flame in the process. That is why God sent Jesus to save us: because we cannot save ourselves. We cannot achieve that bonding on our own. Jesus bestows it upon us when we are ready. We can, however, prepare to be his bride by fulfilling all the requirements of the Law. And we can have faith that when we do fulfill them, we will experience the alchemical marriage that the saints have experienced and described.

We prepare for union with God by praying and invoking the violet flame, by letting go of our imperfections, by giving ourselves in service to God and others, by letting go of things that simply don't matter anymore. Eventually we understand that nothing else matters besides the bonding of our soul to Christ.

And we determine that we will be bonded to Christ. Until we are, our soul does not have the gift of immortal life. Not one of us is guaranteed our ascension. We have no guarantee where we will go after this life when our body no longer serves us. The only guarantee we have is to make our soul immortal through becoming the bride of Christ.

Gifts from the Heavenly Bridegroom

Saint Teresa of Avila recorded that one day in 1572 Jesus gave her his right hand and said, "Behold this nail [that is, the nail print]; it is a sign you will be My bride from today on.... My honor is yours, and yours Mine." A few years later Jesus gave her a ring. She wrote:

> Our Lord told me that since I was His bride I should make requests of Him, for He had promised that whatever I asked He would grant me. And as a token He gave me a beautiful ring, with a precious stone resembling an amethyst but with a brilliance very different from any here on earth."[11]

Jesus also explained to Teresa that, in the true tradition of a marriage union, he would share with her all that was his—both the joys and the burdens. He told her: "Whatever I have is yours. So I give you all the trials and sufferings I underwent."[12]

This is true in any marriage—the union is in sharing all. Ask yourself, are you ready for your Bridegroom? Are you ready for all the joys and the sorrows and the sufferings?

Thérèse of Lisieux wrote of an incident in her life that took place on the day she received the habit of a novice nun. As was traditional, during the Clothing Day ceremony she wore a wedding garment to symbolize her betrothal to Christ. The story reflects her simple, innocent relationship to Jesus:

I had always wished that on the day I received the Habit, nature would be adorned in white just like me. The evening before,…the temperature was so mild I could no longer hope for any snow. The following morning the skies hadn't changed. The celebration, however, was wonderful.…

[After the ceremony,] I entered the cloister once more, and the first thing that struck my eye was the statue of "the little Jesus" smiling at me from the midst of flowers and lights. Immediately afterwards, my glance was drawn to the snow, the monastery garden was white like me! What thoughtfulness on the part of Jesus! Anticipating the desires of His fiancée, He gave her snow. Snow! What mortal bridegroom, no matter how powerful he may be, could make snow fall from heaven to charm his beloved?[13]

Thérèse's story, to me, exemplifies calling upon God, talking to him, telling him the desire of the heart, and then surrendering the matter completely. As Thérèse demonstrates, we must be ready for him to say yes or no or to be silent. Thérèse had simply wished in her heart that it might snow because she loved the snow. She never thought that she deserved that it should snow. She never demanded snow or expected that Jesus should fulfill her desire for snow. And, when she saw the ground white with snow, she took it as a miracle, not as a right.

Bonding with the Heart of Christ

In the unitive stage some mystics have experienced a close bonding of their heart to the heart of Christ. During the last days of her life Saint Gertrude, a thirteenth-century Benedictine nun who had a special devotion to the Sacred Heart of Jesus, saw Jesus open his heart with his hands. Flames shot out and fused her heart to his. A shining silver-and-gold tree grew from the two hearts. Branches from that tree, bearing beautiful fruits, hung over those for whom Gertrude had prayed. Christ told her: "This tree has grown from the union of your will with mine."[14]

A mystic by the name of Sister Barbara heard Jesus say to her: "Thou art all Mine, and I am all thine." She later perceived that he had placed a chain around her heart and attached it to his own heart. She said:

> From that moment I was so bound to my God and so closely united with Him that I can say truly that between God and myself there was but one will.[15]

The beloved Padre Pio wrote in a letter of a profound experience of oneness with Christ:

> When Mass was over, I remained with Jesus in thanksgiving. Oh, how sweet was the colloquy with Paradise that morning. It was such that, although I want to tell you all about it, I cannot. The heart of Jesus and my own—allow me to use the expression— were fused. No longer were two hearts beating, only one. My own heart had disappeared, as a drop of water is lost in the ocean. Jesus was its Paradise, its king. My joy was so intense and deep that I could bear no more and tears of happiness poured down my cheeks.[16]

In the fourteenth-century, mystic Walter Hilton taught that the greater the desire for Christ, the tighter will the bond to him be. He said:

> Jesus is knitted and fastened to man's soul by good will and a great desire for Him alone.... The greater this desire is, the more firmly Jesus is knitted to the soul; the less the desire, the looser the bond. Then whatever spirit or experience lessens this desire and

would draw it down from a steadfast awareness of Jesus Christ and from its natural rising up to Him will unknit and unfasten Jesus from the soul.[17]

We must be in hot pursuit of God, just as he is in hot pursuit of us. We hear the burning intensity in this cry of the psalmist:

As the hart panteth after the water brooks, so panteth my soul after thee, O God. My soul thirsteth for God, for the living God: when shall I come and appear before God?[18]

Active Love, Selfless Love

The most important sign of the mystical union with God is an active love. Of all stages of the mystical path, the unitive stage is the most fruitful. Mysticism is an eager, outgoing activity whose driving power is generous love. It is not our concept of someone withdrawing. It is the active pace that produces power, because it is motivated by the singleness of desire—the desire to love God and to be God. "If...thine eye be single, thy whole body shall be full of light."[19]

Over and over again, the great mystics have told us not how they speculated but how they acted. And in most cases they did not even tell us how they acted; it remained for others to write the inscription of their lives.

As the mystics describe it, the transition from the life of the outer senses to the refined life of the Spirit is a formidable undertaking that demands effort and constancy. Their favorite symbols are those of action, battle, search, pilgrimage, marriage. For them, the quiet of contemplative life is but the outward stillness essential for inward work.

Author Evelyn Underhill noted that prominent early mystics were often referred to as "spiritual athletes." She explains:

It remains a paradox of the mystics that the passivity at which they appear to aim is really a state of the most intense activity: more, that where it is wholly absent no great creative action can take place. In it, the superficial self compels itself to be still, in order that it may liberate another more deep-seated power which is, in the ecstasy of the contemplative genius, raised to the highest pitch of efficiency.[20]

The nineteenth-century French mystic Elizabeth de la Trinité said that in the unitive stage, all the movements of the soul become divine. "Though [the movements of the soul] are God's, they are just as much the soul's," she said. "For our Lord performs them in and with her."[21] Thus the mystic becomes the living instrument of God—the heart, head and hand of God in action. Saint Symeon expressed this eloquently in his "Hymns of Divine Love." He wrote:

We are limbs of Christ; Christ is our limb. And my hand, the hand of the poorest creature, is Christ; and my foot is Christ; and I, the poorest creature, am the hand and foot of Christ. I move my hand, and so does Christ, for he, in entirety, is my hand: You must understand that the Godhead is undivided. I move my foot—it shines as he does.

Say not that I blaspheme, but confirm this and adore Christ, who has made you so. For you too, if you will, can become his limb. And so all the limbs of each of us will become limbs of Christ and Christ will become our limb, and he will make all that is ugly and ill-formed beautiful and well-formed, adorning it with the splendor and dignity of his divinity.

And we shall all together become gods, intimately united with God, aware of no blemish on our bodies, but sharing fully in the resemblance to the entire body of Christ; so each of us shall have all of Christ. For the One, when he has become many, remains One undivided; but every part is the whole Christ.[22]

Teresa of Avila taught that as a result of the spiritual marriage, "the soul is much more occupied than before with everything pertaining to the service of God." All of the energy of the soul who is married to Christ, she said, "goes into finding ways to please him, and into seeing how and where it may show the love it has for him. This is what prayer is for,...and this is the purpose of the spiritual marriage, which gives rise always to works, works!" "Works are what the Lord wants!"[23]

Teresa herself led a very active life, dedicating herself to the reform of the Carmelite Order. Her life offers us a prime example of a life lived in selfless love—and this is yet another way to define a mystic. She traveled throughout Spain, establishing seventeen monasteries, and wrote several books that have become spiritual classics.

In Teresa's day and culture, these accomplishments were nothing less than remarkable. Women were by nature thought to be incapable of higher learning and more susceptible to the wiles of the devil. It was a saying of her time that a woman should only leave the house on three occasions: her baptism, her going to the house of the man she marries, and her burial. In 1970 Saint Teresa of Avila became the first woman to be made a Doctor of the Church.

Many Christs Are Needed

Another active mystic was Saint Catherine of Siena. Catherine is the second woman to receive the title of Doctor of the Church. Catherine's mystical marriage took place in 1366 at the age of nineteen. As she prayed in the little room of her house where she had lived a secluded life for three years, Jesus promised her, "I will espouse you to me in faith."[24] He gave her a gold ring set with four pearls and a diamond and said that this was her reward for scorning the vanities of the world and desiring only him.

Catherine's life changed immediately and she began a career of unceasing service. She left her cell to care for the poor and sick. She preached, traveled widely and addressed hundreds of letters to the prelates and sovereigns of her day, both advising and rebuking them. Wherever she went she brought a spiritual revival.

In the *Dialogue*, the record of Catherine of Siena's conversations with God the Father, the Father taught:

> When the will of the soul "unites itself [with me] in a most perfect and burning love," the soul "is another me, made so by the union of love."[25] "You will know me in yourself," he told her, "and from this knowledge you will draw all that you need."[26]

Jesus taught Catherine that her bonding to him had to bear fruit not only for herself but for other souls as well. He said that she had to fly to heaven on "two wings"—"love of me and love of your neighbor."[27]

For Catherine, "love of your neighbor" consisted of both action and intercessory prayer. God instructed her: "Let not a moment pass without crying out for these others in my presence with humble voice and constant prayer."[28]

One of Catherine's recorded prayers reads:

> Your Son is not about to come again except in majesty to judge.... But, as I see it, you are calling your servants christs, and through them you want to relieve the world of death and restore it to life.
>
> How? You want these servants of yours to walk courageously along the Word's way, with concern and blazing desire, working for your honor and the salvation of souls....
>
> O best of remedy-givers! Give us then these christs, who will live in continual watching and tears and prayers for the world's salvation. You call them your christs because they are conformed to your only-begotten Son.[29]

A Path for Today

Jesus revealed to Catherine of Siena that there must be many Christs. We are all Christs in potential, and the level to which our Christ Self is seated in each one depends entirely upon us and what action each of us takes from this profound understanding.

The practices of the Christian mystics are not only two thousand years old but are as old as the coming of the Word with God in the Beginning. The path that we walk today under Jesus Christ, Saint Germain and the ascended masters is solidly grounded in the ancient traditions, not only of the Christian mystics, but of all the avatars that have ever come to earth.

The mystical path is truly a practical path for today. It is practical because we learn how to contact God and find our way back to his heart. It is practical because it deals with the needs of the hour on planet earth. As Nobel Laureate Dag Hammarskjöld once wrote, "In our era, the road to holiness necessarily passes through the world of action."[30] Thérèse of Lisieux expressed it this way: "Souls that are on fire can never be at rest."[31]

Through our study of Christian mysticism, we have learned something of the path practiced by the saints and ascended masters when they were mystics walking the earth. We have learned that many among the Mystical Body of God have drunk of this cup, bonded with Christ and united with God. Thus, we can have faith that we, too, can drink of this same cup and achieve the same result: union with God.

Prayers and Meditations

Prayer for Christ Wholeness

*In the name of the mighty Presence of God which
I AM and by and through the magnetic power of the sacred
fire vested in the threefold flame burning within my heart,
I decree for Christ wholeness for myself and for all souls
of light:*

1. *I AM God's perfection manifest
   In body, mind, and soul—
   I AM God's direction flowing
   To heal and keep me whole!*

Refrain:
*O atoms, cells, electrons
Within this form of mine,
Let heaven's own perfection
Make me now divine!*

*The spirals of Christ wholeness
Enfold me by his might—
I AM the Master Presence
Commanding, "Be all light!"*

2. *I AM God's perfect image:
   My form is charged by love;
   Let shadows now diminish,
   Be blessed by comfort's dove!*

3. O blessed Jesus, Master dear,
   Send thy ray of healing here;
   Fill me with thy life above,
   Raise me in thine arms of love!

4. I AM Christ's healing Presence,
   All shining like a mercy sun—
   I AM that pure perfection,
   My perfect healing won!

5. I charge and charge and charge myself
   With radiant I AM light—
   I feel the flow of purity
   That now makes all things right!

And in full faith I consciously accept this manifest, manifest, manifest! [repeat the preceding sentence 3 times before continuing:] right here and now with full power, eternally sustained, all-powerfully active, ever expanding and world enfolding until all are wholly ascended in the light and free! Beloved I AM! Beloved I AM! Beloved I AM!

My Life Is Thine

All that I had thought my own—
My name, my fame, my contacts
    (fears and blames)—
I cast them all within thy flame;
And in the glow of mastery
My Christed radiance now I see
Descending from the heart of God,
A special gift of thine own love.

Descending now, thy Presence fair
In answer to my humble prayer
Reveals thyself as light in me;
The presence of eternity
In time consents to honor thee
And be restored to rightful place
Wherein my eyes behold thy face
Appear transcendent as the dawn,
The brightness of a cosmic morn
Where sweet surrender then is born
And consecration comes to me
Forevermore to be like thee.

I AM thyself in action here;
Thy grace, O God, in me appears!
Thy kingdom come—my life is thine—
And thus we triumph over time!

PART THREE

Formulas
for Mystical
Transformation

CHAPTER 14

Becoming God's Heart,
Head and Hand

The ascended master El Morya is a great mystic who, throughout many embodiments, maintained a steadfast devotion to the will of God. He has given us a series of decrees that he called the "Heart, Head and Hand Decrees." These decrees represent the steps, or stages, in the disciplines of the life of Jesus Christ. In them, El Morya has given to us a certain formula that is so profound and powerful and yet so simple. I invite you to give these mantras as I explain the steps and stages of your union with God in them. And I invite you to make them the very first decrees that come into your heart each day when you awaken.

Purification by Violet Fire

The first stage, "Violet Fire," consists of three short decrees for soul-purging and purification—for soul-fasting through the heart, the head and the hand. "Heart" takes in the heart chakra that so yearns to become one with the Sacred Heart of Jesus. "Head" takes in the head, the third eye, the crown and the throat chakras. And "Hand" takes in the secret-ray chakras that are in the hands.

As you accept the violet flame as God and God's emanation of himself and his name I AM, and as you give this decree while so freely feeling your soul's absorption of God, you can become, in a matter of moments, like the lower half of that manifestation of God that forms a complete circle by uniting with the higher half. There's a part of you that is God. It is the seed of light. Your God Presence is above you. Separating you from union with your I AM Presence are doubt and fear, psychological blocks, negative karma. But these things can be set aside for our moments of meditation and we can experience union. And then we can go out more determined than ever to remove the blocks that keep us from twenty-four-hour oneness in God.

As you give these mantras, visualize the violet flame blazing through the heart and the head and being released through the hand in action. "Heart, Head and Hand" is a ritual of the flow of energy. These mantras will quiet the emotions. They will integrate mind, body and soul. And they are for the fulfillment of the self. They free the energies of life.

Say these words as a most profound prayer in which you are speaking to the violet flame as the Holy Spirit and speaking to your I AM Presence and Holy Christ Self. As you say this prayer, feel the tremendous, tangible love and devotion of your heart:

Heart

Violet Fire, thou love divine,
Blaze within this heart of mine!
Thou art mercy forever true,
Keep me always in tune with you.

Head

I AM light, thou Christ in me,
Set my mind forever free;
Violet fire, forever shine
Deep within this mind of mine.

God who gives my daily bread,
With violet fire fill my head
Till thy radiance heavenlike
Makes my mind a mind of light.

Hand

I AM the hand of God in action,
Gaining victory every day;
My pure soul's great satisfaction
Is to walk the Middle Way.

In these mantras we use the name of God "I AM," and when we say I AM, we are affirming "I and my Father are one."[1] Jesus promised us: "I will come again, and receive you unto myself; that where I am, there ye may be also."[2] This means that right where we are, right where we commune with God, there God is.

The Protective Power of Light

The first step, purification, is truly the washing of the four lower bodies with the violet flame. Now that you have done that with the preceding mantras, it is lawful for you to invoke the tube of light. The tube of light is the extension of God's Presence around you.

And so, just as you would not prepare to meet an expected guest without bathing and making yourself presentable and your home tidy, you must also anticipate the coming of the LORD by celebrating those necessary rituals—in this case, most importantly, the violet-flame ablution, the purification that allows you to feel the Presence of God in the tube of light and not just see it as a milky white tube with you inside.

I invite you to stand in honor of your God Presence whenever you give this decree invoking the tube of light. See yourself standing inside a cylinder of light, nine feet in diameter (depicted opposite page 34), that descends from the heart of your God Presence. Sense that God is actually lowering a portion of his Presence upon you. Speak to your mighty I AM Presence as you give this prayer. The more you are in harmony with that Presence, the greater will be your citadel of light.

When I offer this prayer, I add power to the devotion that I am expressing in the decree "Violet Fire." This is because the strength of your tube of light is a matter of your visualization and your will. How much *will* do you have? How much will and determination are involved in your desiring to have this tube of light? How much desire and will do you have to know God and to be one with God?

Your tube of light is sustained in this octave by your will and desire to have it and by your visualization. I visualize every single word that I say in this tube of light decree with all of the power of my being until the tube of light is like steel around me. How much do you want God's protection? That's how much you will put into this call. But always remember: It is love that connects you to God and brings down the tube of light around you. I invite you to give the tube of light prayer with these thoughts in mind:

Tube of Light Decree

Beloved I AM Presence bright,
Round me seal your tube of light

From ascended master flame
Called forth now in God's own name.
Let it keep my temple free
From all discord sent to me.

I AM calling forth violet fire
To blaze and transmute all desire,
Keeping on in freedom's name
Till I AM one with the violet flame.

Having called forth your tube of light, you have set your force-field with God and are communing with him. Decrees are the greatest means of talking with God. When you decree, you are conversing with God. If you are wandering in your mind or looking around the room or thinking about what you're going to do when you finish your decrees, you have lost the greatest blessing of them. Think of decrees as an intimate conversation with God in which you are expressing to him those qualities you desire to strengthen in your life.

Forgiveness Is First and Foremost

First and foremost among God's qualities, we ask for forgiveness. Jesus taught us to pray, "Forgive us our debts, as we forgive our debtors."[3]

Release forgiveness to everyone as you give the forgiveness mantra. Wherever you may have a sense of injustice or that you have been wronged, visualize the violet flame of forgiveness going forth from your heart in this mantra of the spoken Word. Visualize the flame of forgiveness contacting every individual with whom you have ever had a misunderstanding. Feel a tremendous sense of peace, love and resolution. As you send out forgiveness, life truly sends forgiveness back to you.

Before you give the mantra, you may wish to offer a simple prayer such as the one below. If there is any discord in your life, name the problem and the people involved, and pray for mercy's fire to consume the cause, effect, record and memory of all that stands between God in you and God in them.

O Lord, I ask for forgiveness for all sins and all karma. I ask for the violet flame to serve those whom I have wronged and those who have wronged me. I especially ask for _____ [make your personal requests here]. With absolute forgiveness to every part of life, I decree:

Forgiveness Decree

I AM forgiveness acting here,
Casting out all doubt and fear,
Setting men forever free
With wings of cosmic victory.

I AM calling in full power
For forgiveness every hour;
To all life in every place
I flood forth forgiving grace.

The Abundant Life

Abundance is the natural law of life, and Jesus always had the abundance of every good and perfect gift from God. He and his disciples were never wanting and yet they did not live in excess. Jesus came that we, too, might have the abundant life. God has promised to us his infinite supply, so why is it that not all of us are manifesting that?

Jesus teaches us that fear and doubt are the basic cause of poverty, the poverty consciousness, and want. We cannot draw forth abundance and supply if we have fear at conscious or subconscious levels. God has given us the Ten Commandments to keep us in line with our mighty I AM Presence so that the floodgates of heaven can open and give to us all that we need.

Being out of alignment with God can also block supply and abundance. The following conditions are some of the things that can keep you out of alignment with God:

- Being disobedient to his laws
- Confessing a sin to your Holy Christ Self, asking for forgiveness and performing a penance to atone for the sin, but then not desisting from it
- Wanting supply for unlawful things or for things that you want for the wrong reasons
- Quarreling or arguing with someone and then not making things right afterwards
- Allowing discord in your life without striving to resolve the cause of it
- Neglecting to love God with all your heart and soul and mind, keep his commandments, and love your neighbor as yourself

The "Supply Decree" gives you greater accessibility to supply because you have asked for it on the foundation of absolute and total forgiveness of yourself and of everyone who has ever wronged you. So remember, if the answer seems not to be forthcoming, first search your heart and come into alignment. See if you need more love, more self-givingness, or a stronger devotional tie to God. Whatever facilitates your pouring forth devotion, whether it's a certain prayer or a song or a decree, whatever puts your heart on fire for God, do that thing. Keep your love and devotion intense.

Supply, of course, is more than material things. It is the riches of the Spirit, the great teaching of God, the supply of all energy. True abundance is the sense that you are a child of your wealthy Father and Mother, the sense that they love you and want to give you all their riches. Prosperity is your true inheritance. It is health, wealth, happiness, joy, peace, faith, hope, wisdom, and more. It is being in tune with the flow of the universe and being able to accept the abundance of God. Declare your freedom as you talk to God through this decree:

Supply Decree

I AM free from fear and doubt,
Casting want and misery out,
Knowing now all good supply
Ever comes from realms on high.

I AM the hand of God's own fortune
Flooding forth the treasures of light,
Now receiving full abundance
To supply each need of life.

The Blueprint of Perfection

Jesus had the awareness of the inner master as being perfect but he did not hold that law of perfection as exclusive to himself. He taught that the law he demonstrated was available to everyone. He instructed us: "Be ye therefore perfect, even as your Father which is in heaven is perfect."[4]

Regularly giving the "Perfection Decree" helps you realize that you can embrace the law of perfection and the energies of perfection that will transform your life. With this decree, you are calling forth the perfect divine plan and inner blueprint for your life.

Perfection Decree

I AM life of God-direction
Blaze thy light of truth in me.
Focus here all God's perfection,
From all discord set me free.

Make and keep me anchored ever
In the justice of thy plan—
I AM the Presence of Perfection
Living the life of God in man!

In this decree you are declaring, "God in me is the life of God-direction." You are not only affirming God's presence within you but are also calling to God to blaze his light of truth in you. Finally, in the concluding part of the mantra you are affirming, "God in me is the presence of perfection." Because you have combined this affirmation with the name of God, I AM, by cosmic law it must manifest in accordance with God's will.

As you give these mantras, you may feel yourself going up by degrees. Whether you can feel it or not, you are literally ascending by degrees with each mantra. What each one of these decrees does is to establish your acceptability on that plane. Each decree is a next step. When you give these carefully worded mantras with full devotion and when you also fulfill all other requirements of the Law, then you can take the next step. You may even feel yourself rising, becoming lighter.

A New Creature in Christ

The "Transfiguration Decree" is one of the most important calls you can ever make. Each time you give this call there is a subtle change in your being. Whenever you give this call, you are changing and being transfigured. And therefore the forces of darkness that would oppose your Christhood can never find you. This is because the person you were yesterday is nowhere. You are a new person today with a new vibration—a new creature in Christ.

The transfiguration flame does this. The moment you give this mantra, you will be of a different vibration than you were in the moment before giving it. Imagine, if you give this mantra daily, how in a lifetime you can truly become transfigured in the likeness of God.

With each successive mantra, you are drawing forth a greater degree of light. As you become increasingly sensitive, you may actually feel this light building within your body. You may begin to feel the burning in the heart, which the disciples felt on the road to Emmaus when they were near the master but did not recognize him. The burning in the heart indicates the expansion of the threefold flame. It is the sacred fire actually consuming the misqualified energies of fear and hatred and impure motive that often surround the heart.

There is a tremendous joy in this transfiguration mantra because it represents an influx of light whereby the very cells of your body begin to be filled with light and to be flushed of physical as well as mental and emotional toxins. The joy of giving these mantras is the joy of becoming God. You can give this decree with a childlike heart because you feel so loved by God. As you speak the words, you are telling your Father what a wondrous change is happening to you and how happy you are that he has given you this gift of going through a transfiguration.

Transfiguration Decree

I AM changing all my garments,
Old ones for the bright new day;
With the sun of understanding
I AM shining all the way.

I AM light within, without;
I AM light is all about.
Fill me, free me, glorify me!
Seal me, heal me, purify me!
Until transfigured they describe me:
I AM shining like the Son,
I AM shining like the sun!

Restoring Wholeness

The resurrection is a resurgence of God's energy through your being, through your chakras. Jesus restored life to his temple by drawing forth the energies of the resurrection from the I AM Presence. By the meditation of his soul upon his Higher Self, he overshadowed his body until he restored it to life.

Begin your resurrection by the restoration of consciousness, joy, happiness, love, truth. Increase and accelerate God's consciousness within your being until you attain the ultimate victory of your soul's reunion with God.

As you give this mantra, visualize white light coming through you, rising through you as a white fire pulsating from beneath your feet through your consciousness and chakras, creating an energy field that can restore you from sickness to health, from depression to wholeness, from anxiety to joy.

Resurrection Decree

I AM the flame of resurrection
Blazing God's pure light through me.
Now I AM raising every atom,
From every shadow I AM free.

I AM the light of God's full Presence,
I AM living ever free.
Now the flame of life eternal
Rises up to victory.

You Ascend Daily

Each day you can celebrate your ascension and know that a tiny part of you is ascending every time you give the ascension mantra. This is absolutely true. Think of it: You ascend in increments. The ascension is the acceleration of consciousness until, ultimately, the soul reunites with the I AM Presence. As soon as you begin to give this decree, you are accelerating the white light in your aura, preparing for your ultimate union with God.

The people who give these mantras daily are brimming with light and joy. Their energies are up—and this is not a coincidence.

As you say the words of this decree, visualize a sphere of white light enveloping your entire form and being. When you say "I AM the living Christ," you are affirming, "God in me is the living Christ. And that Christ, which was in Jesus, is now manifesting in me as the fullness of the threefold flame in my heart."

Ascension Decree

I AM ascension light,
Victory flowing free,
All of good won at last
For all eternity.

I AM light, all weights are gone.
Into the air I raise;
To all I pour with full God power
My wondrous song of praise.

> *All hail! I AM the living Christ,*
> *The ever-loving One.*
> *Ascended now with full God power,*
> *I AM a blazing sun!*

After you have concluded giving the "Heart, Head and Hand Decrees," seal the action of precipitation with a closing. Doing so causes light to descend tangibly from Spirit into matter:

> *I accept this done right now with full power. I AM this done right now with full power. I AM, I AM, I AM God life expressing perfection all ways at all times. This which I call forth for myself I call forth for every man, woman and child on this planet.*

The Key to Your Mystical Union with God

What I would like to say to you in simple conclusion about your decrees is this: Decrees are the key to your mystical union with God. Whatever you decree, mean it. You will receive the greatest benefit from your decrees when you literally pour yourself, the energies of your being, into them. Make every moment count. Yes, even five minutes at a time will do if you commune with total fervor and fiery dedication, with one-pointed attention on your God Presence, with love for all the hosts of the LORD—no distractions, no stray thoughts, no digressions, just total communion with God. Pour the light of all of your chakras into your moments of communion with God.

Prayers and Meditations

O Living Flame of Divine Love

O living flame of Divine Love, we stand before thee. We bow before thee as the everlasting Light. Divine Love, come forth for our soul's purging, for our soul's illumination, for our soul's union with God. O God, consume all that is not real in us! O thou Divine Light who art Christos in us and all around us, we not only bow before thee but we internalize thy flame. Intensify, O God. Intensify, O God. Intensify, O God.

O God, we call forth the fullness of the cross of white fire. O angels of the cosmic cross, come unto us and minister unto us and let us realize God dominion in this place. O mighty Light, let the fullness of the path of our mystical union with God be made known to us. Strip from us sheaths of mortality, human density, human consciousness. O God, receive us. Thy light is a burning, shining light for the victory of all lightbearers on earth.

Come, Holy Spirit! Come, living flame! We know nothing else but thee, O God. To know thee truly is to be thyself in action. This is our true calling and our reason for being. Therefore, O God, seal our souls in their fiery destiny. Seal us in the name of the Father, the Son, the Holy Spirit and the Divine Mother.

We accept thy Presence with us now. We decree it. We welcome it. We accept it done in the name of Jesus Christ. Amen.

The Peace of Christ

May the peace of Christ surround you
May the peace of Christ abound in you
May the peace of Christ be with you
May the peace of Christ shine forth from you
May the peace of Christ be established upon earth
And may his flame abide in all.

Seraphic
Meditations

Seraphic Meditations

These meditations are to be given as the observations a man would make if he had attained the level of consciousness of the seraphim, the six-winged angels that Isaiah saw hovering above the throne of God.[1] They may be given as a prayer by all who aspire to these heights of glory.

Choose a time when you will not be distracted. Allow the meditations to carry you to a place of profound communion with the Divine. Before beginning, offer a personal prayer entreating the holy seraphim to assist you on your path of purgation, illumination and union—your path to becoming God.

And I beheld the great electronic fire rings of the Great Central Sun. I saw the surface thereof as of molten gold, blending with an azure blue. The sky became a sea and, behold, the soft glow as of pale pink roses of living flame bubbling upon the surface beneath, translucent and then transparent; a white-fire core that pulsed and rose and fell with a holy radiance inundated my soul. My eyes I sought to shield from the glorious wonder which I knew to be reality, infinity and love without end.

All knowledge, all power, all love going on forever and having neither beginning nor ending were before me. And I saw the naturalness of home, of friends, of family, of all that ever was and is or is to come. Ribbons of interconnecting glory from this gigantic orb spread into space from galaxy to galaxy, from star system to star system, and the song of the music of the spheres moved upon the strings of my heart as a lute of fire.

I heard the turning of the seemingly silent spheres and the tones of the cosmic fires, of dead and dying worlds, blended with the nova, the eternally new, the children of space, interstellar systems moving outward into the far-flung deserts where the fractional margins spread apart, yet they were engulfed in the love of the center.

My soul was separated from my body, and I understood that all that I had felt to be a tether of solidity and of identification with an integral, "dyed-in-the-wool" consciousness was no more. I roamed through spiral nebulae, through gossamer veils of light, through the flaming hair of the seraphim. I saw the places of the Sun and the turning of empty worlds as well as those that were overly populated with a progressive order of humanity.

I understood the message of the Elder Ones and I knew that the consciousness of a little child was the consciousness of the innocent of heart. I knew that the pure in heart should see God[2] and that the sophistications of the earth were a curse to my own reality. My heart burst as chunks of ice melted and became a warm liquid that revived all of the hope within my bones.

O Divine Love, thou wouldst not separate me—no, not for an instant—from the experiences of eternity. The last enemy that shall be destroyed is death. O death, where is thy sting? O grave, where is thy victory?[3] I know now no tethers to keep me from thy Presence. Thy majesty with me is every man with me, and I with every man pursue the course that leads to Thee.

Consciousness can move. It can penetrate. It can fly. It can break tethers. It can loose itself from the moorings of life and go out into the sea, the briny deep where the salt tears of my joy are a spume of hope, renewed again and again. I am gladdened as never before, and there is no remembrance of the former conditions. These are put aside as finite, as trite, as a passing fancy of the mortal mind.

Now I engage my consciousness
With the beings of fire,
With the seraphic hosts—
Now I see God's desire
To be the most intense,
Glowing white radiance—
A furnace white-hot
Whose coolness is my delight.

I see the shadows and the veils
Of human thought and human foolishness
Melt and evaporate,
Vanish in the air;
And all that I AM is everywhere
And everywhere I AM.

Consume in me the dross, O God,
The impure substance of the sod,
The dingy state of mortal fame—
Consume it all, O mighty flame,
And take me by the hand right now
And lead me to thy light that glows.

My soul as fairest, sweetest rose
Emits the perfume of creative essence.
Lo, I AM mine own God Presence—
Taken from the flame of truth,
My vital energies of youth,

My infinite strength is holy proof
That as thou art I, too, shall be—
Removed from all impurity
Until thy very face I see.

I AM the pure in heart,
For the pure in heart shall see God.
And as I join hands
With seraphic bands,
I know that out from the world of illusion,
Confusion, commercialization,
Unrealization, intense prudery,
And retreating fear of the light,
I AM come!

I have overcome fear and doubt.
I stand now clothed upon
With a garment spun of the Sun—
My flesh is clothed with an Electronic
Swaddling Garment:
It electrifies my entire form;
It renews my mind,
My identity with its original self,
And the glow of that Star
That is within me and on my forehead
Is one of hope for the ages.

I come under thy dominion
And all things come under my dominion.
I AM the Lord thy God,
The Lord thy God I AM—
For between the shores of our being

There is oneness,
The oneness of hope that does evoke
A release from all that is not real.

By thy grace, O God, I am made to feel
I am made to heal!
I am made to seal myself
And all that I am
Within a garment of electronic light
Whose impenetrability, bright radiance,
Shining down the dawn of foreverness,
Refuses acceptance
Of any mortal thought whatsoever
That limits my soul,
For by thy grace I am made whole.
Out of the Light I am come
And with Thee I am unified to see
Shining down the century,
The corridor of years, of light
Of *pralaya*, of mantrams, prayers,
And ended human tantrums—
The celestial manifestation
Of God terrestrial
Raised unto the heaven-world
Where the ascension currents,
As electronic essence,
Pursue in me every dark chasm
And intensification of mortal passion
Until they are milked—
Placed in the violet-fire caldrons—
And purified as substance of shining light.

O God, here am I, here I AM!

One with thee and One to command
Open the doorway of my consciousness
And let me demand as never before
My birthright to restore.

Thy prodigal son has come to Thee[4]
And longs once again to walk with Thee
Every step of the way Home.

NOTES

Transformation into Christ through Prayer
by Blessed Angela of Foligno
1. Angela of Foligno, *Complete Works*, trans. Paul Lachance (Mahway, N.J.: Paulist Press, 1993), p. 287.

PRELUDE   To Souls Yearning to Be One with God
1. *The Book of Her Life* 20.13, in *The Collected Works of St. Teresa of Avila*, trans. Kieran Kavanaugh and Otilio Rodriguez, 3 vols. (Washington, D.C.: ICS Publications, 1976-85), 1:133. Subsequent references to these volumes are cited as *Collected Works*.
2. Raymond Bernard Blakney, *Meister Eckhart: A Modern Translation* (New York: Harper and Brothers, 1941), p. 180.
3. John G. Arintero, *The Mystical Evolution in the Development and Vitality of the Church*, trans. Jordan Aumann, 2 vols. (St. Louis, Mo.: B. Herder Book Company, 1949), 1:38, 23.
4. Ibid., p. 39, n. 68.
5. Matt. 5:48. All Bible references are to the King James Version.
6. Summit University is a school of personal transformative learning on the frontier of religion, science and culture. Programs include online study courses, weekend seminars, and longer programs covering one or more in-depth topics in a unique spiritual environment.
7. *Book of Her Life* 20.10, in *Collected Works* 1:132.
8. Thomas Merton, *The New Man* (London: Burns and Oates, Continuum, 1976), p. 80.

CHAPTER 1　An Experience That Transforms the Soul

1. Robert A. Vaughan, *Hours with the Mystics: A Contribution to the History of Religious Opinion* (1856; reprint, n.p., Kessinger Publishing, 1992), p. 175.

2. Michael Cox, *A Handbook of Christian Mysticism*, rev. and exp. (Great Britain: Aquarian Press, Crucible, 1986), p. 130; Arthur L. Clements, *Poetry of Contemplation: John Donne, George Herbert, Henry Vaughan, and the Modern Period* (Albany, N.Y.: State University of New York Press, 1990), p. 16.

3. *Dionysius the Areopagite: The Mystical Theology and the Celestial Hierarchies* (1949; reprint, n.p., Kessinger Publishing, 2003), p. 9.

4. Exod. 3:13–15.

5. Exod. 20:6.

6. John 14:15, 21, 23; 15:10; I John 5:3; II John 1:6.

7. Jer. 23: 5, 6; 33: 15, 16.

8. Exod. 3:14, 15.

9. Author Philip St. Romain writes: "There is nothing in Christian teaching comparable to the Hindu notions of chakras…. Neither will one find in Christianity anything like the spiritualities associated with the yoga system, which are designed to lead one up through the various centers to the experience of union. Nevertheless, the chakras…[and other] experiences…can be identified in the experiences of many, many Christian mystics" (*Kundalini Energy and Christian Spirituality* [New York: Crossroad, 1991], pp. 74–75).

10. *St. Thérèse of Lisieux, Her Last Conversations*, trans. John Clarke (Washington, DC: ICS Publications, 1977), p. 102; *Story of a Soul: The Autobiography of St. Thérèse of Lisieux*, trans. John Clarke (Washington, D.C.: ICS Publications, 1976), p. 263.

11. Henry Thomas and Dana Lee Thomas, *Living Biographies of Great Scientists* (Garden City, N.Y.: Nelson Doubleday, 1941), p. 15.

12. Ibid., p. 16.

CHAPTER 2   God Dwells within You

1. I Cor. 3:16.
2. John 14:23.
3. Rom. 8:6, 14, 16, 17.
4. II Pet. 1:4.
5. Sidney Spencer, *Mysticism in World Religion* (1963; reprint, Gloucester, Mass.: Peter Smith, 1971), p. 245; Meister Eckhart, *Sermons and Treatises*, trans. and ed. M. O'C. Walshe (Longmead, Shaftesbury, Dorset: Element Books, 1987), 3:107.
6. Joseph James, arr., *The Way of Mysticism* (New York: Harper and Brothers Publishers, n.d.), p. 64.
7. Oliver Davies, *God Within: The Mystical Tradition of Northern Europe* (New York: Paulist Press, 1988), p. 48.
8. Eckhart, *Sermons and Treatises* 3:107.
9. Gal. 2:20.
10. Gal. 4:19.
11. Col. 1:27.
12. Hans Urs von Balthasar, ed., *Origen: Spirit and Fire; A Thematic Anthology of His Writings*, trans. Robert J. Daly (Washington, D.C.: Catholic University of America Press, 1984), p. 270.
13. Spencer, *Mysticism in World Religion*, p. 250.
14. Ibid., p. 285.
15. Ibid., pp. 286, 287.
16. Rom. 8:26, 27.
17. Exod. 26:31–34; Lev. 16:1, 2; Heb. 9:1–8; 10:14–22.
18. Matt. 27:50, 51; Mark 15:37, 38; Luke 23:45, 46.
19. John 1:9.

CHAPTER 3   The Rebirth of the Mystical Path

1. I Cor. 2:6, 7, 9, 10, 16.
2. Isa. 55:1–3, 6–8, 11–13.

CHAPTER 4   Mystical Contemplation and Prayer

1. John Climacus, *The Ladder of Divine Ascent* (Mahwah, N.J.: Paulist Press, 1982), p. 274.
2. *The Story of a Soul: The Autobiography of St. Therese of*

Lisieux, ed. T. N. Taylor (1912; reprint, n.p., CreateSpace, 2010), pp. 134, 133.

3. Francisco de Osuna, *The Third Spiritual Alphabet*, trans. Mary E. Giles (New York: Paulist Press, 1981). p. 45.

4. *Book of Her Life* 8.5, in *Collected Works* 1:67.

5. *The Way of Perfection* 26.9, in *Collected Works* 2:136.

6. Holmes Welch, *Taoism: The Parting of the Way*, rev. ed. (Boston: Beacon Paperback, 1966), p. 69.

7. Therese of Lisieux, *Story of a Soul*, ed. T. N. Taylor (n.p., Biblio-Life, 2008), p. 166.

8. Walter Hilton, *The Stairway of Perfection*, trans. M. L. Del Mastro (Garden City, N.Y.: Doubleday and Company, Image Books, 1979), p. 77.

9. Climacus, *Ladder of Divine Ascent*, p. 280.

10. Arintero, *Mystical Evolution* 2:118, 119.

11. Exod. 20:3, 5; 34:14.

12. The *Interior Castle* 1.1.1, in *Collected Works* 2:283.

13. Ibid., 7.2.3; 1.1.3, pp. 433, 284.

14. Ibid., 1.1.7 , p. 286.

15. *Saint Germain On Alchemy: Formulas for Self-Transformation* (Gardiner, Mont.: Summit University Press, 1993), pp. 350–52.

16. Spencer, *Mysticism in World Religion*, p. 227

17. Geneviève of the Holy Face, *My Sister Saint Thérèse* (1959; reprint, Rockford, Ill.: Tan Books and Publishers, 1997), p. 104.

18. Brother Lawrence, *The Practice of the Presence of God, with Spiritual Maxims* (Grand Rapids, Mich.: Baker Book House Company, Spire Books, 1967), pp. 12, 30.

19. *The Book of Her Foundations* 5.8, in *Collected Works* 3:119–20.

20. I Thess. 5:17.

21. Ps. 42:1–3, 9–11.

CHAPTER 5   Forging Christhood

1. *The Collected Works of St. John of the Cross*, trans. Kieran Kavanaugh and Otilio Rodriguez (Washington, D.C.: ICS Publications, 1973), p. 295.

2. *The Ascent of Mount Carmel* 2.5.7; 2.7.8, in *Collected Works of*

222 🔥 *Notes to Pages to 69–86*

St. John of the Cross, pp. 117, 124.

3. See Ezek. 1:4.

4. Evelyn Underhill, *Mysticism: A Study in the Nature and Development of Man's Spiritual Consciousness* (1911; reprint, New York: E. P. Dutton and Company, 1961), pp. 181–82.

5. Catherine of Genoa, *Purgation and Purgatory, The Spiritual Dialogue*, trans. Serge Hughes (New York: Paulist Press, 1979), p. 81.

6. I Cor. 15:31.

7. Catherine of Genoa, *Purgation and Purgatory*, pp. 79–80.

8. Ibid., p. 29.

9. Ibid., pp. 29–30.

CHAPTER 6   The Dark Night of the Senses

1. E. W. Trueman Dicken, *The Crucible of Love: A Study of the Mysticism of St. Teresa of Jesus and St. John of the Cross* (New York: Sheed and Ward, 1963), pp. 127, 223, 294, 258.

2. *Ascent of Mount Carmel* 1.2.1, in *Collected Works of St. John of the Cross*, p. 74.

3. Ibid.

4. Ibid., p. 75.

5. Dicken, *Crucible of Love*, p. 223.

6. Mary Baker Eddy, *Science and Health with Key to the Scriptures* (Boston: First Church of Christ, Scientist, 1971), p. 494.

7. *Ascent of Mount Carmel* 1.13.11, in *Collected Works of St. John of the Cross*, p. 103.

8. F. C. Happold, *Mysticism: A Study and an Anthology*, rev. ed. (Harmondsworth, Middlesex, England: Penguin Books, 1970), p. 359.

9. John 14:12.

10. Happold, *Mysticism*, p. 359.

11. *Ascent of Mount Carmel* 1.10.1, in *Collected Works of St. John of the Cross*, p. 94.

12. Luke 9:23; Matt. 16:24.

13. Luke 9:24; Matt. 16:25.

14. Gal. 6:2.

15. Arintero, *Mystical Evolution* 2:126.
16. Gal. 6:4, 5.
17. Heinrich Seuse, *The Exemplar: Life and Writings of Blessed Henry Suso*, vol. 1 (n.p.: Priory Press, 1962), p. 38.
18. John 14:20.

CHAPTER 7   An Accelerated Path
             to Soul Freedom

1. Thomas R. Nevin, *Thérèse of Lisieux: God's Gentle Warrior* (New York: Oxford University Press, 2006), p. 271; http://www. ewtn.com/library/MARY/THERESE.HTM
2. Fritjof Capra, *The Tao of Physics*, 2nd ed. (New York: Bantam books, 1984), p. 141.
3. Deut. 4:24.
4. Luke 3:16; Matt. 3:11; Mark 1:7–8; John 1:33.
5. Isa. 1:18.
6. Matt. 18:19, 20.

CHAPTER 8   Fasting on the Spiritual Path

1. Climacus, *Ladder of Divine Ascent*, pp. 256, 169.
2. *Francis and Clare: The Complete Works*, trans. Regis J. Armstrong and Ignatius C. Brady (New York: Paulist Press, 1982), p. 214.
3. Ilias the Presbyter, *A Gnomic Anthology* 1:57, in *The Philokalia: The Complete Text*, vol. 3, comp. St Nikodimus of the Holy Mountain and St Makarios of Corinth (London: Faber and Faber, 1984), p. 40.

CHAPTER 9   Visions and Revelations

1. Arintero, *Mystical Evolution* 2:43, 44.
2. Sergius Bolshakoff, *Russian Mystics* (Cisterian Publications, 1980), pp. 35–36.
3. Paul E. Szarmach, ed., *An Introduction to the Medieval Mystics of Europe* (Albany, N.Y.: State University of New York Press, 1984), p. 164.
4. *The Life of Saint Teresa of Ávila by Herself*, trans. J. M. Cohen

(London: Penguin Classics, 1957), p. 285.

5. *Book of Her Life* 27:6, in *Collected Works* 1:176.

6. Balthasar, *Origen: Spirit and Fire*, p. 234.

7. E. Le Joly, *Servant of Love: Mother Teresa and Her Missionaries of Charity* (San Francisco: Harper and Row, 1977), p. 17.

8. H. A. Reinhold, ed., *The Soul Afire: Revelations of the Mystics* (Garden City, N.Y.: Doubleday and Company, Image Books, 1973), pp. 333–35.

9. *Book of Her Life* 27.2, in *Collected Works* 1:174.

10. Ibid., 27.3, p. 175.

11. *Interior Castle* 7.1.8, in *Collected Works* 2:431.

12. *Book of Her Life* 10.1, in *Collected Works* 1:74.

13. Ibid., 20.5, p. 130.

14. Harvey Egan, *An Anthology of Christian Mysticism* (Collegeville, Minn.: Liturgical Press, Pueblo Book, 1991), p. 358.

15. J. Mary Luti, *Teresa of Avila's Way* (Collegeville, Minn.: Liturgical Press, Michael Glazier Book, 1991), pp. 10–11.

CHAPTER 10   Experiences of the Mystics

1. The phrase "the highest school that exists in the world" is taken from Ray C. Petry, ed., *Late Medieval Mysticism* (Philadelphia: Westminster Press, 1957), p. 259.

2. Seuse, *The Exemplar*, pp. 49–50.

3. See Mark L. Prophet and Elizabeth Clare Prophet, *The Masters and Their Retreats* (Gardiner, Mont.: Summit University Press, 2003).

4. *Book of Her Life* 32:11, in *Collected Works* 1:217; Cox, *Handbook of Christian Mysticism*, p. 163.

5. *Spiritual Testimonies* 48, in *Collected Works* 1:345.

6. Seuse, *The Exemplar*, pp. 107–8.

7. *The International Thesaurus of Quotations*, comp. Rhoda Thomas Tripp (New York: Harper and Row, 1970) , no. 86.8, p. 55.

8. *Barnes and Noble Book of Quotations*, rev. and en. (New York: Harper and Row, Barnes and Noble Book, 1987), p. 367.

9. Björn Landström, *Columbus* (New York: Macmillan Company,

1966), p. 152.
10. Ibid., p. 170.
11. Ibid., pp. 170–71.
12. Ibid., p. 171.
13. Ibid., pp. 172–73.

CHAPTER 11   Illumination through Revelation

1. *The Prayers of Catherine of Siena*, ed. Suzanne Noffke 2nd ed. (New York: Paulist Press, 1983), p. 104.
2. Spencer, *Mysticism in World Religion*, p. 213.
3. Seuse, *The Exemplar*, p. 14.
4. *Book of Her Life* 31.11, in *Collected Works* 1:207.
5. Reinhold, *Soul Afire*, p. 136.
6. Spencer, *Mysticism in World Religion*, pp. 225, 226.
7. Arintero, *Mystical Evolution* 2:97, note 5.
8. Ibid.
9. Reinhold, *Soul Afire*, pp. 336, 337.
10. Matt. 19:27.
11. Mark 10:29–31.
12. Louis Dupré and James A. Wiseman, eds., *Light from Light: An Anthology of Christian Mysticism* (New York: Paulist Press, 1988), p. 218.
13. Matt. 23:37.
14. *Time*, 25 May 1992, p. 23.
15. Catherine of Siena, *The Dialogue*, ed. Suzanne Noffke (Mahwah, N.J.: Paulist Press, 1980), p. 179.
16. Duprè and Wiseman, *Light from Light*, pp. 216, 217.
17. Ibid., pp. 217, 220.

CHAPTER 12   Spiritual Betrothal

1. Walter T. Stace, ed., *The Teachings of the Mystics* (New York: New American Library, Mentor Book, 1960), p. 184.
2. Egan, *Anthology of Christian Mysticism*, p. 511.
3. *Soeur Thérèse of Lisieux, The Little Flower of Jesus*, ed. T. N. Taylor (New York: P. J. Kenedy and Sons, 1924), p. 195.
4. *Story of a Soul: The Autobiography of St. Thérèse of Lisieux*,

trans. John Clarke, 2nd ed. (Washington, D.C.: ICS Publications, 1976), p. 194.

5. *Book of Her Life* 29.13, in *Collected Works* 1:194.
6. Arintero, *Mystical Evolution* 2:284.
7. Catherine of Genoa, *Purgation and Purgatory*, pp. 16–17.
8. *The Living Flame of Love* prologue 3–4; stanza 1 commentary, in *Collected Works of St. John of the Cross*, pp. 578, 580.
9. *The History and Life of the Reverend Doctor John Tauler, with Twenty-five of His Sermons*, trans. Susanna Winkworth (1905; reprint, Kessinger Publishing, 2007), p. 290.
10. Arintero, *Mystical Evolution* 2:195, n. 41.
11. *Dark Night* 2.5.1, in *Collected Works of St. John of the Cross*, p. 335.
12. John of the Cross, *Dark Night of the Soul* 2.6.5, 6, trans. E. Allison Peers (n.p.: Doubleday, Image Books, 2005), p. 68.
13. Matt. 27:46; Mark 15:34.
14. John 19:30.

CHAPTER 13   The Soul's Spiritual Marriage to Christ
1. Evelyn Underhill, *The Essentials of Mysticism* (1920; reprint, New York: Cosimo, n.d.) , p. 71.
2. *Spiritual Canticle* 26.14, in *Collected Works of St. John of the Cross*, p. 514.
3. Gal. 2:20.
4. Arintero, *Mystical Evolution* 2:38.
5. Egan, *Anthology of Christian Mysticism*, p. 215.
6. Vaughan, *Hours with the Mystics*, p. 175.
7. Stace, *Teachings of the Mystics*, pp. 184–85.
8. Spencer, *Mysticism in World Religion*, p. 254.
9. Michael Freze, *They Bore the Wounds of Christ: The Mystery of the Sacred Stigmata* (Huntington, Ind.: Our Sunday Visitor Publishing, 1989), p. 206.
10. Arintero, *Mystical Evolution* 2:171, n. 3.
11. *Spiritual Testimonies* 31, 34, in *Collected Works* 1:336, 337.
12. Ibid., 46, p. 344.
13. Thérèse of Lisieux, *Story of a Soul*, pp. 154, 155–56.

14. Mary Jeremy Finnegan, *Scholars and Mystics* (Chicago: H. Regnery Company, 1962), p. 205.
15. Arintero, *Mystical Evolution* 2:171, n. 3.
16. Eileen Dunn Bertanzetti, *Praying in the Presence of Our Lord with St. Padre Pio* (Huntington, Ind.: Our Sunday Visitor Publishing, 2004), pp. 67–68.
17. Hilton, *Stairway of Perfection*, p. 76.
18. Ps. 42:1, 2.
19. Matt. 6:22; Luke 11:34.
20. Underhill, *Mysticism*, p. 50.
21. Spencer, *Mysticism in World Religion*, p. 255.
22. Martin Buber, comp., *Ecstatic Confessions: The Heart of Mysticism*, ed. Paul Mendes-Flohr, trans. Esther Cameron (Syracuse, N.Y.: Syracuse University Press, 1996), pp. 38–39.
23. *Interior Castle* 7.1.8, in *Collected Works* 2:430; Dicken, *Crucible of Love*, p. 429; *Interior Castle* 5.3.11, in *Collected Works* 2:352.
24. Raymond of Capua, *The Life of Catherine of Siena*, trans. Conleth Kearns (Wilmington, Del.: Michael Glazier, 1980), p. 106.
25. Egan, *Anthology of Christian Mysticism*, p. 361.
26. Mary Ann Fatula, *Catherine of Siena's Way*, rev. ed. (Wilmington, Del.: Michael Glazier, 1989), p. 80.
27. Raymond of Capua, *Life of Catherine of Siena*, p. 116.
28. Catherine of Siena, *The Dialogue*, trans. Suzanne Noffke (New York: Paulist Press, 1980), p. 32.
29. *The Prayers of Catherine of Siena*, ed. Suzanne Noffke (New York: Paulist Press, 1983), pp. 178, 179.
30. Dag Hammarskjöld, *Markings*, trans. Leif Sjöberg and W. H. Auden (New York: Alfred A. Knopf, 1965), p. 122.
31. *Soeur Thérèse of Lisieux*, p. 176.

CHAPTER 14   Becoming God's Heart, Head and Hand
1. John 10:30.
2. John 14:3.
3. Matt. 6:12.
4. Matt. 5:48.

Seraphic Meditations

1. Isa. 6.
2. Matt. 5:8.
3. I Cor. 15:55.
4. Luke 15:11–32.

SELECTED BIBLIOGRAPHY

Angela of Foligno. *Complete Works*. Trans. Paul Lachance. Mahwah, N.J.: Paulist Press, 1993.

Arintero, John G. *The Mystical Evolution in the Development and Vitality of the Church*. Trans. Jordan Aumann. 2 vols. St. Louis, Mo.: B. Herder Book Company, 1949.

Balthasar, Hans Urs von. *Origen, Spirit and Fire: A Thematic Anthology of His Writings*. Trans. Robert J. Daly. Washington, D.C.: Catholic University of America Press, 1984.

Bolshakoff, Sergius. *Russian Mystics*. N.p.: Liturgical Press, Cisterian Publications, 1977.

Brother Lawrence. *The Practice of the Presence of God, with Spiritual Maxims*. Grand Rapids, Mich.: Baker Book House Company, Spire Books, 1967.

Catherine of Genoa. *Purgation and Purgatory, The Spiritual Dialogue*. Trans. Serge Hughes. New York: Paulist Press, 1979.

Catherine of Siena. *The Dialogue*. Trans. Suzanne Noffke. Mahwah, N.J.: Paulist Press, 1980.

———. *The Prayers of Saint Catherine*. Ed. Suzanne Noffke. New York: Paulist Press, 1983.

Climacus, John. *The Ladder of Divine Ascent*. Trans. Colm Luibheid and Norman Russell. Mahwah, N.J.: Paulist Press, 1982.

Cox, Michael. *A Handbook of Christian Mysticism*. Great Britain: Aquarian Press, Crucible, 1986.

Davies, Oliver. *God Within: The Mystical Tradition of Northern Europe*. New York: Paulist Press, 1988.

Dicken, E. W. Trueman. *The Crucible of Love: A Study of the Mysticism of St. Teresa of Jesus and St. John of the Cross.* New York: Sheed and Ward, 1963.

Dupré, Louis and James A. Wiseman, eds. *Light from Light: An Anthology of Christian Mysticism.* New York: Paulist Press, 1988.

Eckhart, Meister. *A Modern Translation.* Trans. Raymond Bernard Blakney. New York: Harper and Brothers, 1941.

———. *Sermons and Treatises.* Trans. and ed. M. O'C. Walshe. 3 vols. Longmead, Shaftesbury, Dorset: Element Books, 1987.

Egan, Harvey. *An Anthology of Christian Mysticism.* Collegeville, Minn.: Liturgical Press, 1991.

Fatula, Mary Ann. *Catherine of Siena's Way.* Rev. ed. Wilmington, Del.: Michael Glazier, 1989.

Francis and Clare: *The Complete Works.* Trans. Regis J. Armstrong and Ignatius C. Brady. New York: Paulist Press, 1982.

Happold, F. C. *Mysticism: A Study and an Anthology.* Rev. ed. Harmondsworth, Middlesex, England: Penguin Books, 1970.

Hilton, Walter. *The Stairway of Perfection.* Trans. M. L. Del Mastro. Garden City, N.Y.: Doubleday and Company, Image Books, 1979.

James, Joseph, arr. *The Way of Mysticism.* New York: Harper and Brothers Publishers, n.d.

John of the Cross. *The Collected Works of St. John of the Cross.* Trans. Kieran Kavanaugh and Otilio Rodriguez. Washington, D.C.: ICS Publications, 1973.

Landström, Björn. *Columbus.* New York: Macmillan Company, 1966.

Luti, J. Mary. Teresa of Avila's Way. Collegeville: Minn.: Liturgical Press, 1991.

Nevin, Thomas R. *Thérèse of Lisieux: God's Gentle Warrior.* New York: Oxford University Press, 2006.

Osuna, Francisco de. *The Third Spiritual Alphabet.* Trans. Mary E. Giles. New York: Paulist Press, 1981.

Raymond of Capua. *The Life of Catherine of Siena.* Trans. Conleth Kearns. Wilmington, Del.: Michael Glazier, 1980.

Reinhold, H. A., ed. *The Soul Afire: Revelations of the Mystics.* Garden City, N.Y.: Doubleday and Company, Image Books, 1973.

Spencer, Sidney. *Mysticism in World Religion.* 1963. Reprint, Gloucester, Mass.: Peter Smith, 1971.

Stace, Walter T., ed. *The Teachings of the Mystics.* New York: New American Library, Mentor Book, 1960.

Szarmach, Paul, ed. *An Introduction to the Medieval Mystics of Europe.* Albany, N.Y.: State University of New York Press, 1984.

Teresa of Avila. *The Book of Her Life.* Trans. Kieran Kavanaugh and Otilio Rodriguez. 1995. Reprint, Indianapolis, Ind.: Hackett Publishing Company, 2008.

———. *The Collected Works of St. Teresa of Avila.* Trans. Kieran Kavanaugh and Otilio Rodriguez. 3 vols. Washington, D.C.: ICS Publications, 1976–85.

Thérèse of Lisieux. *Soeur Thérèse of Lisieux, The Little Flower of Jesus.* Ed. T. N. Taylor. New York: P. J. Kenedy and Sons, 1924.

———. *Story of a Soul: The Autobiography of St. Thérèse of Lisieux.* Trans. John Clarke. 2d ed. Washington, D.C., ICS Publications, 1976.

Underhill, Evelyn. *The Essentials of Mysticism.* 1920. Reprint, New York: Cosimo Classics, n.d.

———. *Mysticism: A Study in the Nature and Development of Man's Spiritual Consciousness.* New York: E. P. Dutton and Company, 1961.

Vaughan, Robert Alfred. *Hours with the Mystics: A Contribution to the History of Religious Opinion.* 1856. Reprint, n.p.: Kessinger Publishing, 1992.

PICTURE CREDITS

Related reading...

Reincarnation: The Missing Link in Christianity
by Elizabeth Clare Prophet
This groundbreaking work traces the history of reincarnation in Christianity. The author argues persuasively that Jesus was a mystic who taught that our destiny is to unite with the God within.

The Lost Years of Jesus: Documentary Evidence of Jesus' 17-Year Journey to the East
by Elizabeth Clare Prophet
Pocketbook or 1-DVD album entitled *The Lost Years and the Lost Teachings of Jesus.* An original lecture by Mrs. Prophet before a live audience.

Titles in the Mystical Paths of the World's Religions series:

Kabbalah: Key to Your Inner Power
by Elizabeth Clare Prophet
Trade paperback book or 4-DVD album of Mrs. Prophet's original lecture before a live audience.

The Buddhic Essence: Ten Stages to Becoming a Buddha
by Elizabeth Clare Prophet
Trade paperback book or 1-DVD album of Mrs. Prophet's original lecture before a live audience.

Becoming God: The Path of the Christian Mystic
by Elizabeth Clare Prophet
Trade paperback book or 3-DVD album of Mrs. Prophet's original lecture before a live audience.

Find all of the above and more at
www.SummitUniversityPress.com
1-800-245-5445 • 406-848-9500

OTHER TITLES FROM

SUMMIT UNIVERSITY ꙮ PRESS®

MYSTICAL PATHS
OF THE WORLD'S RELIGIONS
Becoming God: The Path of the Christian Mystic
The Buddhic Essence: Ten Steps to Becoming a Buddha
Kabbalah: Key to Your Inner Power

RELATED TITLES
Fallen Angels Among Us: What You Need to Know
Fallen Angels and the Origins of Evil
Reincarnation: The Missing Link in Christianity
Mary Magdalene and the Divine Feminine
The Lost Years of Jesus

POCKET GUIDES
TO PRACTICAL SPIRITUALITY
I Am Your Guard
Is Mother Nature Mad?
The Story of Your Soul
Your Seven Energy Centers
Karma and Reincarnation
The Art of Practical Spirituality
How to Work with Angels
Creative Abundance
Soul Mates and Twin Flames
Alchemy of the Heart
The Creative Power of Sound
Access the Power of Your Higher Self
Violet Flame to Heal Body, Mind and Soul

For More Information

Summit University Press books and products are available at fine bookstores worldwide and online at your favorite bookseller and at www.SummitUniversityPress.com.

To download a free catalog of Summit University Press books and products, please visit our Web site.

Summit University Press
63 Summit Way, Gardiner, MT 59030 USA
Tel: 1-800-245-5445 or 406-848-9500
Fax: 1-800-221-8307 or 406-848-9555
www.SummitUniversityPress.com
info@SummitUniversityPress.com

ELIZABETH CLARE PROPHET is a world-renowned author. Among her bestselling titles are *Fallen Angels and the Origins of Evil, The Lost Years of Jesus, Reincarnation: The Missing Link in Christianity, Kabbalah: Key to Your Inner Power* from the Mystical Paths of the World's Religions series, and her Pocket Guides to Practical Spirituality series, which includes *Your Seven Energy Centers, Karma and Reincarnation, The Story of Your Soul,* and *Violet Flame to Heal Body, Mind and Soul.*

Mrs. Prophet has pioneered techniques in practical spirituality, including the creative power of sound for personal growth and world transformation.

A wide selection of her books has been translated into a total of 29 languages worldwide.

The unpublished works of Mark L. Prophet and Elizabeth Clare Prophet continue to be published by Summit University Press.